Also by Eric Henze

The Complete Guide to Henry Cowell State Park (coming 2015)

A Family Guide to the Grand Circle National Parks

RVing with Monsters

All titles published by Gone Beyond Guides

Find us on Facebook and Twitter!

 facebook.com/GBG.GoneBeyondGuides

 twitter.com/GoneBeyondGuide

THE COMPLETE GUIDE TO
WILDER RANCH STATE PARK

Eric Henze

Gone Beyond Guides
Publisher

You can reach the author through our FaceBook page:
www.facebook.com/GBG.GoneBeyondGuides

ISBN-10: 0989039218

ISBN-13: 978-0-9890392-1-5

To Bonny Hawley with gratitude and much appreciation

Contents

Acknowledgements

Acknowledgements are typically read only by those being acknowledged, so out of respect for each of them, here's a little more, here are the people that really made this book happen.

First day I mentioned to the Wilder Staff I was writing a book, I ran into Bill Perry. Bill is 88 years old and proud of it, as he should be because he gives monthly hiking tours and is a man to keep up with! Sharp of wit, with a kind smile and a subtle wisdom in the way he carries himself, Bill took me in and showed me the land of Wilder. He brought a lot of detail to the geology and lime kiln sections of this book as well as a few jokes.

When I asked to speak to a docent to verify the historical content in this book, everyone threw out Pat Kennedy as the resource to meet. I went to introduce myself during one of the park events and didn't really think this through as I had never seen her before and there were probably 600 people visiting the ranch property that day. I was told she couldn't be missed because she was the "only red haired docent". That was enough detail because she was and I found her. Pat has played a huge part in this project providing fact checking, little details and the ever gentle, "I'm sure you omitted this on purpose but what about....?" details. Pat and her fellow docent friends have a book of their own, called Wilder Ranch State Park Cookbook 1870's to the 1920's. It's in the bookstore and to be honest, I bought it but purposely did not read it simply because the book also contains some stories of Wilder and I didn't want to take away from what they have created. (If you've read both and I did end up duplicating stories, it wasn't intentional Pat!)

Bonny Hawley is the Executive Director of the Friends of Santa Cruz State Parks. I dedicated this book to Bonny as this is my first book and she was instrumental in helping me ensure its completion. She believed in the project, believed in me and my sucess as an author begins with Bonny's faith and support. We first met to discuss the project over coffee at Lulu Carpenters at the

Octagon in downtown Santa Cruz. I was met by a warm friendly soul who sat and patiently listened to my passionate ramblings for the better part of an hour. I went in with very little expectations to be honest and left becoming a part of Friends of Santa Cruz State Parks, to which I am humbly honored.

I've asked a few people to read over my book before putting it in the hands of the public. As a writer, the hardest thing to do is to get a friend to say something bad about your stuff. Most people will read it, that's the easy part, but getting them to give constructive criticism is another thing. These folks were good enough friends to move beyond the pleasantries of political correctness and give some hard critical feedback. Now that's a friend you want to have beside you for life. To Bata Ng, Portia Halbert, Lee Summers, Ernest Doucette, Dayna Langone and George Trager, what can I say but I love you. I guess I can say one more thing, thanks to each of you for making this book a better read!

I want to thank Ken Sievers who contributed many of the photos for this guide. When I first met Ken, I wondered if he wasn't a now humbly retired but once famous movie actor, he just has that charismatic persona. Ken's eye captures some of the essence of Wilder through his photos.

I want to send out a special thanks to Associate State Archeologist Mark Hylkema. While there is a good deal of information on the Ohlone, the details are either absent or varied. Mark's in depth knowledge and expertise not only provided a singular beacon of truth, but brought needed context to the people behind the culture. Mark was instrumental in helping to present the Ohlone correctly.

I also want to acknowledge all the time I stole from my two boys Everest and Bryce as well as my wife Angela to create this book. Fatherhood is a precious gift and each moment both good and bad is to be cherished. The saying that they grow up so fast is about as true a saying as there ever was and so it was with some mixed feelings to use some of that time to write this book. Everest and Bryce, this book is ultimately for you, your generation and the generations that you will take a part in creating one day.

If you've gotten this far, see, the Acknowledgement section doesn't have to be dry and part of some inner circle. In fact, there is one more acknowledgement I need to make and that is to you, the Reader. Whether you bought, borrowed, stole, copied or read this as an excerpt on the internet, I want to thank you. The goal of this book is singly purposed, to increase adoption of one of the best State Parks in California, Wilder Ranch State Park. If you are reading this, then you are a part of that goal and thus a part of history. Enjoy, thanks and again, thank you!

Introduction

It is said that there is a time and place for all things. For Wilder there is its present condition as an absolutely stunning 7,000 acre California State Park set aside for all to enjoy. A causal hiker can meander along a sea bluff of the rugged North Coast, a mountain biker can get lost in the coastal hills above the bluffs and equestrians can sit atop their four legged companion and watch the ocean spread out before them as their horse climbs up the chaparral.

There were times however that the land called Wilder was something different, in fact, it was many things before it became a State Park. It was a cattle ranch and a dairy ranch. It was a setting for lime kiln factories and lumber mills. Going further back it was the home of a Russian otter trader, a man who would leave his home country and start anew as a Mexican citizen. It was once part of the lands belonging to the Spanish missionaries. It was home to wildlife and foul and fish that were so abundant it astounded early settlers. It was the home of a complex civilization, the Ohlone, who lived with the land for over 10,000 years. It has seen itself touched by no one, cultivated by the Ohlone, exploited by no less than three countries and only recently, protected.

There are some 55 major plant species within the park and 35 mammals. There is a preserved dairy ranch that one can explore. There is surfing for the surfers and a great example of marine terracing for the geographers. Perhaps most importantly though, there are the stories of the people that helped shape what we know as Wilder Ranch State Park.

All of this is what makes up The Complete Guide to Wilder Ranch State Park. Read on!

General
Information

Getting There

Wilder Ranch State Park is located 1.8 miles past the Western Drive spotlight north of Santa Cruz or 4.9 miles south of Davenport directly off Highway 1. To get there from the South Bay Area, travelers can take Highway 17 South toward Santa Cruz. Merge onto Highway 1 north staying generally to your right through Santa Cruz to Wilder. Alternately, you can take Highway 92 South to Half Moon Bay and turn left heading south along Highway 1. The park's entrance is on the coastal side of Highway 1 and is well marked. Parking is just above the historic ranch complex and Interpretive Center.

Highway 17 is known for its twists and turns through redwood forests which while scenic, is a highway frequented by accidents. Both Highways get loaded with beach traffic on weekends which can dramatically slow traffic. Highway 1 from Highway 92 is typically longer so allow extra driving time.

Wilder Ranch State Park is located at 1401 Old Coast Road, Santa Cruz, CA 95060.

Parking

Just after the entrance toll gate there is ample parking at the main lot. Alternatively, there are several areas to park and enter the park for free scattered along the highway (some are described in detail under Surfing). Parking in the main lot is $10 and is typically safe from theft, whereas parking along Highway 1 is free, albeit commonly picked over by thieves.

Another great reason to pay for parking is that a portion of the fee goes directly to Friends of Santa Cruz State Parks, which means the funds are kept locally to aid the park directly.

Gas, Food, Lodging

Santa Cruz offers a wide array of gas, food and lodging for tourists. Food variety is plentiful in Santa Cruz, ranging from well-known fast food establishments to exotic independent fare. If you do drive through Highway 1 north past the UC Santa Cruz campus, you may notice many restaurants with lines literally out the door with students hitting up local eats. Most of these are quite good but expect a wait.

North of Wilder is Davenport, a small town of 408 residents with one or two of everything in the category of gas, food and lodging.

Operating Hours, Amenities and Telephone

Wilder Ranch is open from 8am to sunset daily. The Park is for day use only and there are no campgrounds or campfires allowed in the park. The exception to this is the horse camp. See section titled Dogs, Horses, Hikers and Mountain Bikes for more information on the horse camp.

Amenities include restrooms, limited food and drinks at the Interpretive Center, a small interpretive center and bookstore, picnic areas and very knowledgeable interpreters and docents.

The Park Store and Interpretive Center, located in the historic bungalow, houses a small but high-quality selection of cultural information and artifacts as well as local history and geological books including a cookbook written by the park interpreters. The park store hours are typically Thursday through Sunday from 10am -4pm. They are closed Thursdays from December through February.

Telephone: 831-423-9703, interpretive Center: 831-426-0505

Fees

Fees are $10 per car and otherwise as stated below.

Handicap Accessibility

Most of the historic ranch is accessible via short ramps with some assistance potentially required. The parking and restroom in the main lot are handicap accessible. Access to the ranch complex and Interpretive Center is available as well. Lifts have been installed to allow access into both the Meder House and the Victorian home. Call the park for details.

Dogs, Horses, Hikers and Mountain Bikes

Dogs are not permitted within Wilder Ranch State Park, with the exception of guide and service dogs.

Equestrians are permitted on all trails through the park with the exception of any that are on the coastal side of Highway 1. There are six horse camps available on a first come, first served basis. Horse camping is $20/night per site. Call the main Wilder Ranch number at 831-423-9703 for access. The horse camps are located just off of Dimeo Lane north of the Park entrance.

Hiking and mountain biking is permitted on every trail in the park. Wilder is a haven for mountain bikers and is considered by some to be the best in the area. For the most part Wilder has a highly courteous mix of hikers and bikers.

Weather by Season and Recommended Clothing

The Bay Area has a mild climate averaging 50-70 °F (10 – 20 °C) year round. Coastal weather can be drastically different than what is found "over the hill" along the San Francisco Bay. Typically coastal weather in general can be foggier, windier and often cooler, even when the bay itself is hot and sunny. It's best to check local weather conditions before heading out and bring layers and a windbreaker along.

What to Do, See and Know

With 7,000 acres and some 34 miles of hiking trails that cover five major ecosystems, Wilder Ranch State Park has a lot to offer its guests. The park is open to hiking, biking and equestrian users, taking them along coastal bluffs, up into oak chaparral and prairie grasslands valleys extending into redwood and mixed evergreen forests.

The park is a historical, agricultural and natural preserve. Once the site of the ranch that supplied the Santa Cruz Mission, it went on to become a working dairy ranch owned by Deloss D. Wilder and family. The historic homes, gardens, and many of its out-buildings still stand today as a historical preserve. Tours and exhibits are available with some frequency; check the Wilder Ranch State Park home events page for more information (California State Parks - Wilder Ranch).

Docents will sometimes dress in period clothing, reenacting customs and operations as they were performed during the late 1800's and early 1900's. The cultural preserve center includes three restored workshops run by water-power, ranch buildings and rodeo arena in addition to the main farm house, Victorian and Interpretive Center. Period cars and tools are on display along with live chickens, horses and vegetable gardens.

Agriculturally some of the land is leased to farmers (who actively produce 12% of our nations Brussels sprouts). Other vegetables and some cattle grazing occur in selected pockets of the park as well.

Within the Park is also a model natural preserve - the entire Wilder Beach is closed to human activity to allow for the restoration of wetlands, native vegetation and nesting grounds for the Snowy Plover. It is difficult to imagine, but Wilder Beach was once an agricultural field. From 1992 - 1994, the Benthic Lab group did thorough research to determine present and past ecological conditions. Since 1994, the Wilder Beach Natural Preserve has been restored to allow both native plants and the threatened Snowy Plover a chance to recover. Today it is easy to imagine what this section of the California coast must have looked like 500 years ago thanks to this restoration effort.

Geology

Geographic view of Wilder Ranch, showing the marine terraces

It is difficult to imagine the immense changes on what seems an unchanged land. Certainly if you look into the hills from the Ohlone Bluff Trail, you are gazing on a view that is little changed since before the arrival of the Spanish Missionaries. However, the land you stand on began in the South Pacific and travelled past present Los Angeles to its present place. The sand of Wilder beaches began in part as the massive granite citadels of the Sierras, broken by wind and water, washed down from the Sacramento Delta under the Golden Gate Bridge and slowly deposited south by ocean currents. While it is difficult to imagine, immense change is exactly what took place to arrive at the present Wilder Ranch State Park.

During the peak of the Pleistocene Ice Age when the oceans were starved by the massive glaciers in the mountains, the shoreline was some 7 miles further into the ocean from where it stands today. Once the Ice Age period ended and the waters were once again allowed to flow to the sea, the unimaginable flows created wide canyons such as what is now known as Wilder Beach.

There are seven marine terraces that make up Wilder all created during the Pleistocene Epoch. If you ever want to refer to someone as really old, "epoch" is a great word for it, as the Pleistocene Epoch started some 2.5 million years ago ending just 12,000 years ago. This time was one of repeated glacial events where water was locked up as ice, released as liquid only to be locked up again as the earth's climate cycled from warmer to colder. At its peak, over 30% of the entire earth was covered with ice. For the more temperate lands of Wilder it meant that with the repeated glaciation, the oceans receded and rose slowly over this vast period of time. The land too took part in the change, moving upwards at 0.6mm per year as well as northwards. As the land rose and the oceans ebbed and flowed, the marine terraces were very literally created like large steps that appeared to move inland as the next one was created.

Each terrace is created first by erosion of a rocky coast line, such as the one currently being formed at Ohlone Bluff. The sea retreats, creating a shore-line while the land is constantly moved upward by tectonic forces (enormous earth plates running into each other). A relative change in the sea level leads to further onslaughts on the next cliff face the upheaval has presented it with and thus begins the formation of another terrace. This of course takes a tremendous amount of time and while it has been studied, there are no conclusive answers as to how long the Wilder Terraces took to be formed.

A great example of recent geology can be found at the Ohlone Bluff Trail at Old Cove Landing. At the back of the cove is a nice sea cave, which in modern times has not been touched by the sea but was created many years past. If you take the trail back towards the Visitor Parking lot 100 yards from this cave you will see a similar sea cave currently being created by the ocean.

Area History

This section gives a summary of Wilder history. If you are looking for more in depth accounts of the people and the historical backstory, look in the Wilder Stories- The People of Wilder section.

Native People

Prior to American settlers, the Spanish, Mexican and even Russian cultures, there was the Ohlone culture. The name "Ohlone" is used today to collectively describe the many different tribes who lived in what is commonly referred to as the San Francisco Bay Area and Monterey. They fished, hunted, harvested, married, traded and were members of sophisticated kinship and alliance networks. They had a high degree of ornamentation in dress and custom as well as rich soulful ceremonial practices. They held in deep and complex spiritual traditions, with their own creation stories, accords on living with each other and with the land in which they lived. They believed in the existence of spirit animals and had their own notion of what happens to a person in the afterlife. They believed in a Great Spirit, and prayed with native tobacco, blowing smoke to Esmen, the Sun. Within the Bay Region, there were some 40 different communities, each with its own leader, territory and often very unique sub cultures.

Archeological dating puts the Ohlone people in the Monterey Bay Area from as early as 7000 BC. Other places in California date back as far as the Ice Age, 10-16,000 years ago, although evidence of such an early presence has been obscured by rising sea levels and environmental changes. The Ohlone held a strong spiritual bond with the land and with each other. The Ohlone are known for their active management of the land and they learned to perform controlled burns and other techniques to increase production of game and harvestable plants. As a result when the Spanish arrived in 1769, they were met with an abundance of wild life, which was due in large part to their active management of the natural resources. Grizzly bears, elk and pronghorn, steelhead and rockfish, sea weeds, mollusks were plentiful. Various waterfowl populated the land amongst massive stands of old growth redwoods and other trees. Along the oceans, sea lions were in such vast quantity that they "looked like pavement", according to early Majorcan missionary and European explorer, Juan Crespi.

Early Sketch of Oholone at the Mission San Jose

Archeologists have pieced together a fascinating depth to the Ohlone culture and overwrites the initial characterization by the early Spaniards. What is most amazing is their deep respect for natural forces and their skills with land management that came through a deep understanding of the environment in which they lived.

An interesting cultural aspect, similar to ours, is that their societies could accumulate wealth. There were tribes who were wealthy and those that were poor. Like all monetary systems, there are a few physical assets that defines the standard for wealth. For the Ohlone, their wealth revolved around the Olive snail shells (Olivella) and the production of high quality crafts like baskets and finely feathered dance aprons and headdresses. Also, exotic materials like obsidian traded from very distant sources were actively bartered.

There is evidence that the tribes within the interior of Central California grew to see the Olivella shell as a statement of wealth. These shells had no dietary significance but are found at archeological sites as beaded necklaces and ornaments. Abalone (Haliotis) was also a symbol of wealth. The Olive snail shell held particular importance to coastal tribes as it is found only in localized coves. This put those tribes that controlled the location of these coves in a unique position of wealth and political power.

There was also ranking within each village, which was made up of a network of clans. Clan members ascribed to different clubs or societies. There was a membership initiation, payment of dues through shell beads and sponsorship of ceremonial events. Each membership had its own unique costumes, customs and obligations to the village. Abalone shell pendants often denoted badge and rank.

The various organizations worked together as a society overseeing the storage and distribution of food, construction of village buildings, and planning the hunting strategies and logistics. They kept track of the seasonal cycles and gave consul on when to relocate within their territories.

Other artifacts that have been found also tell of sophistication. They created pitted stones for tenderizing shellfish and fashioned both grooved stone weights, shell and bone fishhooks fishing.

The Ohlone that occupied the area from Davenport to Aptos was made up of 5 communities, with the Uypi being the polity that extended from Wilder Ranch to Santa Cruz. Middens found today show that the ancestral Ohlone people had villages at Wilder Ranch proper. The Ohlone would make Tule boats from the extensive wetlands in the area

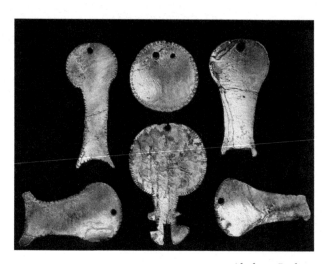

Abalone Badges

(most of which are gone today) to fish and gather marine fowl and mammals. They enjoyed a rich abundance of wildlife for the almost 6000 years they inhabited the region. Even when settlers came to the region, the abundance of fowl in the wetlands was so extensive that "when alarmed by a rifle shot they would rise in a dense cloud with a noise like that of a hurricane".

The Ohlone maintained and in some cases increased this abundance through active management of the land through tilling, pruning, coppicing and fire. (Coppicing is a woodland management practice of harvesting from species of trees that create new growth from the stumps of the original tree). These actions not only elevate the Ohlone above being strictly hunter gatherers but are challenging the definition of agriculture itself amongst researchers.

The area around Wilder just prior to the Spanish arrival is believed to have looked similar to what you would see today. There are accounts of Spanish cattle grazing the same hillside pastures that Wilder and other dairymen would leverage later on. The most notable difference would be an expanse of old growth forests, extensive wetlands and a much larger abundance of wildlife and native flora during the heyday of the Ohlone as compared to a visit to the Wilder lands today.

When the Spanish arrived in 1769, there were many thousands of people living in the Bay Area. Their stability and complex infrastructure was interrupted with disastrous results for the people. The mission of Santa Cruz was one of seven missions built under the direction of Junipero Serra with the objective of establishing a chain of missions to populate the territories to create a colonial foothold on the empire's far flung frontier by converting the Ohlone and other native peoples to Christianity. The missions actively acted to disrupt the social structure and overall Ohlone culture. Many of the Ohlone were moved to the missions where they faced overcrowding and then subsequent disease, infant mortality and miscarriages that led to a spiral of brutal demise for the people. In one incident in the spring of 1806, the native culture lost over one quarter of their population to a measles outbreak.

By 1834 the Mexican government secularized the missions and the Ohlone people. While now in a less controlled state, they watched as their land was divided again into vast Mexican owned rancherias. By this time, it is estimated that the Ohlone population was a mere 10 percent of what it was prior to the Spanish arrival. The remaining Ohlone men became the ranch hands and cowboys that worked the land owned by the Rancheria owners. When the Gold Rush came in 1848, the California population boomed bringing a new wave of ethnic discrimination that pushed the Ohlone population further into decline and near extinction. The Ohlone were stewards of a more balanced natural world for thousands of years. After all that time, in just 58 years their culture would be changed forever.

The Ohlone still survive today. For the most part they continue to practice and retain many of the beliefs and ceremonial structures that had served them prior to the Spanish, Mexican and American occupation. The remaining Ohlone are currently striving to get the United States' Bureau of Indian Affairs to recognize them as a federally recognized tribe.

Rancho del Refugio

The land that is now Wilder Ranch State Park passed through a number of hands before becoming what the park it is today. The Ohlone culture were custodians of the land for thousands of years. Then as the world was being discovered the Spanish took first control of what would become California. Even during the Spanish arrival to California, there was a northward migration of Mexican citizens as well. The Mexicans were called Californios and the land where they lived was Alta California.

As the Mexicans quietly moved northward, the Spanish were boldly standing up a line of missions that started in San Diego moving as far north as Sonoma. One mission that held particular significance to Wilder is Mission Santa Cruz.

The Mission Santa Cruz had a vast livestock grazing area called the Rancho Arroyo del Matadero or "ranch of the streambed slaughtering ground". In possession from 1791 to 1835, the mission encompassed all land west of the Mission. This was one of many large ranchos the mission system set up and was devoted primarily to raising cattle and sheep.

Things changed in 1821 when Mexico gained independence from Spain. With growing insurgence, the Mexican people had enough of the Spanish and engaged in ten years of civil war to acquire their independence. California, which was seen as a high water mark in the Spanish conquests, would also prove to be a costly venture to maintain and as part of the agreement, ownership of "Alta California" was transferred to the Mexican Government. Monterey was made the state capital of Mexico's new state. In 1833, the new government ordered the secularization (decommissioning) of the missions and the entire Rancho Arroyo del Matadero was repossessed, leaving the mission padres with only the church, the priest's quarters and the humble priest's garden. The ranch fell into the hands of Jose Joaquin Castro.

In 1838 Señor Castro died of smallpox and his daughters were subsequently granted the property by the Mexican Government. The ranch was renamed "Rancho Refugio" (Refuge Ranch) and the three daughters Maria, Jacinta Antonia, and Maria de Los Angeles enjoyed their 12,147 acre inheritance until the United States gained control of California during the eighteen month conflict known appropriately as the Mexican – American War in 1848.

A young man by the name of Osip Volkov would jump ship in Monterey, defect from his mother country of Russia, change his name to Jose Bolcoff, become a Mexican citizen, marry Maria Castro and ultimately take ownership of Ranch Refugio giving title ultimately to his two sons. The back story of Osip is one of the more interesting aspects of Wilder history and reads like a daytime soap opera. It is detailed in the Wilder Stories section.

When the Mexican – American War ended, these two sons, Juan and Francisco Bolcoff, were able to retain the ownership claim to the land. However, this came at a huge financial cost in legal fees. In 1854, Jose defaulted on a loan to local businessman, Moses A. Meder resulting in Moses taking control of two-thirds of the Rancho Refugio. The land passed through the hands of another land mogul, John T. Fairbanks who then sold 4,160 acres to Deloss D. Wilder and Levi K. Baldwin in 1871.

It is unknown just how much either Wilder or Baldwin knew about the rich and tarried history of the land they had purchased. What is clear is they just wanted to be successful dairymen making the finest butter in the region.

D.D. Wilder's Creamery

Wilder Creamery

It is said that at the height of the California Gold Rush, there were at times a "continuous line of wagons" moving west from the Mississippi River. California grew from a small languid territory of 1500 people to over 300,000 residents within a year of the discovery. San Francisco boomed from 200 people in 1846 to around 36,000 by 1852. The Gold Rush meant opportunity and not just because of the gold.

Deloss D. (D.D.) Wilder came late to the Gold Rush, arriving in California in 1853. He like others fell under the spell of placer mining and endured the seven month journey from his home in Connecticut across the plains to Placer County. D.D. was of farming stock and understood hard work. He mined the gold fields with little success for almost six years before turning his sights and meager profits towards Marin County.

In Marin, Wilder went from gold miner to chicken and dairy farmer, working on a patch of leased land. There he found greater success than he had as a miner, both as a farmer and in love, meeting his wife, Miranda Finch, formerly from Michigan. They married in 1867 and began to dream of taking dairy farming to a larger scale. Levi K. Baldwin was another dairy farmer in Marin and he shared the same dream.

Wilder and Baldwin found cheap land in Santa Cruz. In 1871, D.D. and Levi purchased 4,030 acres of some of the finest dairy land in the world. Baldwin had earned quite a reputation for his butter and brought that skill to Santa Cruz. Both Baldwin and Wilder hauled butter by ship to the growing population of San Francisco and surrounding areas.

The partnership was not a lasting one and in 1885 Baldwin and Wilder decided to split their acreage into two tracts. The two went to the top of a hill and divided the land by eye. Then they flipped a coin with the winner being able to choose which half to take. D.D. Wilder won the toss and was able to acquire the lower tract of 2,330 acres while Baldwin took the upper portion of the farm with the cattle divided equally between the two.

The farm under Wilder's full control flourished. The primary farm house had twenty rooms, with a barn built later that was large enough to keep 200 cows dry at night plus another barn for up to 15 horses. The property also housed a blacksmith shop, wagon house, machine shop, two granaries and the center of operations, the massive creamery. In the long shadows of late afternoon, one would have seen some 300 cattle coming home to be milked. Milk and cream were sold wholesale while butter was their chief product.

One of the most innovative aspects of the ranch was that the majority of the operation was powered by water. From the small Wilder Creek, the water was diverted to a holding pond uphill from the property. The dam then released a steady stream of water falling some 216 feet. This gravity fed force created from the creek was ample enough to turn several Pelton wheels. Each wheel was struck by the force of the water and spun, powering a generator and many other items of machinery. The generator could produce 100 horsepower of energy. It ran the 150 lights on the farm but even more ingenious, he used the energy to create large lighting arcs that simulated the sunrise to the cows. Each day this artificial sunrise woke them up so they could be milked earlier than normal. These small but mighty streams of water ran the cream separators, the lathes, a churn, a wood saw, wood planer, cabinet saws, feed cutter and pumpkin grinder amongst a list of other items. The power was used efficiently on the farm and was rarely let go to waste.

Picture of the lighting that brought an "early sunrise" to the cows

The farm was passed down for five generations. The success brought them a new Victorian style home in 1897 that D.D. built for his son Melvin. Unfortunately, the ranch was put up for sale in 1969, when the property taxes on the land exceeded farm income. There were a few years where the land almost became a housing

The Pelton Wheel at Wilder Ranch

development, but the good citizens of Santa Cruz County rose up in opposition. In 1974 the California State Parks established Wilder State Park.

In 1996, the California State Parks system acquired the adjacent Gray Whale Ranch through a purchase by the Save-the-Redwoods League. Today the park consists of 7000 acres and is one of the best examples of historical, marine and native plant preservation in the State Park system.

Adams Creek Lime Kilns

While on a walking tour of Wilder Ranch, park docent Bill Perry told me about the "Three L's" of Santa Cruz's heyday of the 1800's; these being lumber, leather and lime. Lumber and leather made sense as there were plenty of trees and cows in the area, but lime? Santa Cruz County was actually the largest lime producer in California with lime kilns scattered throughout the region. The biggest of them all, Adams Lime Kiln, was located right here in Wilder Ranch State Park.

While the process for making lime and its use is amongst the oldest in the chronicles of human civilization, dating back some 7,000 years, most modern wanderers have no idea how to make it nor why it is valuable. Lime is made by heating limestone, marble or any raw material containing calcium carbonate to 1640° F. Doing so drives out the carbon dioxide; leaving lime, (calcium hydroxide) a white, caustic material that acts violently with water. Lime as a word was originally a term for "stickiness", which is appropriate since if you add lime with sand and then add water, you get mortar. Prior to the invention of Portland cement beginning in 1824, lime based mortar was the standard stuff put between bricks for buildings in San Francisco and elsewhere. A thinner mixture was used as plaster as well.

The lime industry was eventually shut down due to the scarcity of cheap firewood. The British invention of Portland cement had an impact too, which remains the standard for making concrete even today. Though it was invented early in the 1800's, it would take over 90 years for Portland cement to completely take hold of the mortar industry. As a result, lime production in Santa Cruz was widespread until the early 1900's. Most of it was shipped to San Francisco by schooners where it was transported by land to help stand up the many gold mining and other towns in California.

Adams Creek Lime Kiln Ruins on Long Meadow Trail

The lime kiln ruins that run along the Long Meadow Trail were originally built in 1858 by Samuel Adams. His lime works were among the largest in Santa Cruz. Samuel employed 38 workers, five of which did nothing but make the wood barrels used to transport the lime. There were 4 kilns in total which allowed for continuous operation. At any given time, one was being loaded, one was burning away at 1640° F, one was cooling and one was being cleaned.

The process for making lime was fairly simple. A "Blaster" would blow up the rock from the limestone quarry. Then several men would take sledgehammers to the rock, creating manageable pieces the size of a melon. The stone was carried by wagons on a makeshift rail system to the kilns. Once loaded, the kiln was heated for four days and required up to 100 cords of wood. It was then allowed to cool for two days before the newly produced lime was loaded into barrels and transported to waiting schooners.

The Adams Kiln operation lasted from 1858 to 1869. Business was not always friendly. Fellow lime industrialist Henry Cowell (of Henry Cowell State Park fame) owned similar lime works within the boundaries of UC Santa Cruz. Cowell would not allow Samuel Adams to access the shorter route up what is now Chinquapin Trail down to port in Santa Cruz.

Instead Adams was forced to go down to Old Cove Landing along the Ohlone Bluff Trail. Henry Cowell would eventually buy out the Adams' Kilns and operate it until about 1909 when the lime industry of Santa Cruz no longer could stand up against the superior Portland cement. Approximately 25% of total lime production during this period came from the Adams Kilns.

An interesting side note, D.D. Wilder never saw the lime traffic through his property as he bought it two years after Adams had sold to Cowell. Cowell by that time was utilizing the shorter route he had denied to Adams to transport his lime.

Gray Whale Ranch

The former Gray Whale Ranch is now the northern portion of Wilder Ranch State Park and starts at Long Meadow Trail ending at Empire Grade adjacent to the UC Santa Cruz campus. The 2,305 acres (9.33 km2) contains the ruins of the Adams Lime Kilns. The land was undeveloped for many years though it was zoned for logging. Given its proximity to both the UC Campus trails and the State Park, there was an assumption by residents that the land would remain as it is today. However, in 1988 local hikers noticed some of the large redwoods tagged to be cut. Apparently the land was being sold and the new owners had filed a Timber Harvest Plan (THP) with the county.

Santa Cruz locals created a "Save the Gray Whale Parklands" campaign and gathered over 4,000 signatures opposing both the development of the land and the Timber Harvest Plan itself. During this time the Chinquapin Trail was actually guarded by hired hands of the new owners, who apparently had plans not only to clear cut the area but build homes. They would soon find that trying to develop land that sat between a state park and college campus was not good business.

The dispute was heavily engaged on both sides with the locals even writing a protest song to aid in their campaign. The County found itself in a battle between approving the THP and development plans for the new owners and keeping the locals who wanted to maintain the area from development happy. When the Save-The-Redwoods League offered to purchase the land in 1996 as "a nice legacy to others", the new owners caved in to the public outcry and sold it to the League for $13.4 million dollars. Escrow closed in 1997 and the land was annexed to the state to become a welcome addition to Wilder Ranch.

Wilder Stories: The People of Wilder

This section provides more detail and depth to the people of Wilder. Herein are stories of greed, determination, happiness, suffering, loss and elation with one thing in common, they all lived in what we now call Wilder Ranch State Park.

Osip Volkov (aka Jose Antonio Bolcoff)

Osip is probably the most notable character beside D.D. Wilder himself and his son Melvin. Here's a guy who comes over from Kamchatka Russia aboard a merchant ship as a teenager, decides to defect into a country that while still owned by the Spanish was five years into a war with the Mexican government. It is interesting to imagine what Osip must have felt on the day his ship sailed back to Russia in 1815 without him.

Osip was baptized at the Mission Soledad in 1817. He would bide his time until 1821 when the Mexican's gained their independence from Spain. During this time he realizes if he wants to stay in "Alta California", he will need to become a Mexican citizen. To do so meant a drastic transformation for the man. He changed his name, his language, his religion and also married into the Mexican bloodline. By 1822, Osip would be forever known as Jose Antonio Bolcoff, would become a Catholic, learn to speak Spanish and marry Maria Candida Castro, one of the three daughters of the prominent ranchero owner Joaquin Castro.

By 1833 the mission properties were dissolved by the Act for the Secular-ization of the Missions of California. While the intent of the secularization was to give the land back to the Ohlone people, many of the Ohlone were never even told of this intent and instead, much of the land would be grant-ed to claims made by Mexican's living in the area. In 1839, the three Castro daughters, (Bolcoff's wife Maria Candida, Maria de Los Angeles, and Jacinta Antonia) made a request for the land that once served as the ranch lands for Mission Santa Cruz.

Jose Bolcoff was appointed administrator of the Mission Santa Cruz from 1822-1839. While it is considered historical gossip that he used his title to grant the lands to the three sisters, the lands were granted to them and they renamed the area Rancho Refugio. Even more interesting, while the original deed named the three sisters as the land owners, the final title that was actual-ly recorded held only one name, Jose Antonio Bolcoff.

Jose would be appointed three separate times as mayor of the town of Bran-ciforte (now a part of Santa Cruz) beginning in 1817. During this time and through to 1854, Jose also ran multiple business ventures on the land. He ran a saw mill with partners Eli Moore and John Doak. The saw mill, built in 1849, was one of the earliest mills in the Santa Cruz region. As is related later in this story, Jose would fall on desperate times and had the saw mill convert-ed to a flour mill just before losing his property in 1854.

During these times he was also able to run another side business, smuggling. The import taxes into Monterey Bay ran between 40% and 100% depending on the product being brought in. The area now known as Sand Plant Beach was in those days nicknamed Smugglers Cove. For a small fee Bolcoff would allow smugglers to bring in their goods via rowboats up the creek to the road under the cover of darkness. Jose would get caught several times and eventu-ally stopped the practice.

Perhaps one the most under told aspects of Jose was his contribution of bring-ing one of the first dairy farms to California. During this period, the range cattle were poor milk producers and were instead bred almost exclusively for their leather, meat and tallow. The concept of running a dairy farm was quite unusual in those days with the only other dairy farm being within the Russian Fort Ross. Osip, also from Russia, had learned the same skills of butter mak-ing in his homeland and brought them to Rancho Refugio.

Jose and Maria would end up having seventeen children, eleven of which survived. When the United States took over California from the Mexican Government, it became a costly endeavor to prove land ownership. Jose would eventually take out a $2,000 mortgage from Moses Meder, who had an interest in obtaining a saw mill of his own. When the original debt could not be paid, Jose took out another mortgage from Moses for an additional $5,000. In the end, Moses Meder foreclosed on the Rancho Refugio in 1854. Meder who took full control of the property and effectively ended the Hispanic occu-pation of the land.

On the Wilder property lies one of the four original adobe structures owned by Jose still stands. In fact it is said that many of the roofing tiles came from Mission Santa Cruz.

Deloss D. Wilder and Levi Baldwin, Partners in Butter

Deloss, also known as D.D., was born in 1826 in West Harland, Connecticut during the presidency of the sixth United States President, John Quincy Adams. In almost every story told of D.D., he is characterized as a man of great strength and character. In Connecticut, he worked for $6.50 per month as a farmer laborer, earning half in cash and half in "store pay".

When D.D. was 27 he finally succumbed to the stories he had heard for over four years about how easy it was to make it rich in the California gold fields. He spent seven months crossing the plains and while he did have some luck placer mining in the Sierra foothills, he would eventually head for the coast of Marin and take up chicken and dairy farming.

It was in Marin that he met up with Levi K. Baldwin, who had experience in the process of making butter, which he shared with D.D. Wilder. The partnership between the two deepened and they both decided to make a larger claim in Santa Cruz purchasing 4,030 acres and began operations of one of the best known dairy-making operations in the Bay Area.

D.D. Wilder was the first of four generations of Wilders to live on the ranch. This section of "Wilder Stories" includes stories from all four, which are:

D.D. Wilder – 1st generation

Loss Wilder – 2nd generation

D.R. Wilder – 3rd generation

Dee Wilder – 4th generation

Elliot's Santa Cruz County Illustrations (1879) describes the butter making process in some detail:

"On a visit to the celebrated dairy of Baldwin and Wilder, we obtained the following information in regard to the manufacture of this noted butter. Mr. Baldwin was an old resident of Marin County, California, extensively engaged in making butter, which was surpassed by none as is well shown by the butter being sold in Washington market, San Francisco since 1858. The market stall has often changed hands, during this time, but the occupants were always anxious to obtain the products of this dairy, which was put up in packages of about four and a half pounds, of square form, and for which, after the first two years the owner of the stall always allowed him the highest market price and charged no commission.

His mode of manufacture is to keep the milk at room temperature so as to allow the milk change in about 36 hours, after which the cream is taken from the milk before the milk gets thick, as he has found by experience that the only way to make good, sweet butter, of fine quality and grain is to take the cream from the milk as soon as the milk is changed.

Baldwin's mode of manufacture has been to temper his cream before churning by setting the cans near fire. After churning, the buttermilk is rinsed from the butter and salt is worked in thoroughly at the rate of 1 pound to 20, and the next day work just enough to mold and cloth it, and immediately put in a box ready for market.

Messrs. Baldwin and Wilder have built a dairy house sufficient for the milk of 250 cows at one time. Milk is strained into a large tank in a room outside, where it is partially cooled before going into the milking room. From this, it is drawn from a faucet extending through a partition into the milk room. The milk is put into ten quart pans set full. In the height of the season, about 600 pans are set per day. The capacity of the churn is sufficient for 280 to 300 pounds of butter, which is from the cream of one day and is churned by horse-power using a box churn.

Baldwin's celebrated butter bears his own private brand, stamped upon one end of each package or square. All sold without this brand is not genuine."

Levi Baldwin

Baldwin and D.D. operated a successful butter making dairy farm from 1871 to 1885 under the Baldwin brand. After 14 years, the two decided to dissolve the partnership and they rode up to a high point on the ranch and divided it in half by eye. They decided to flip a coin to decide the fate of the land and D.D. won, obtaining the lower half. He paid $32,000 (about $14 per acre) for the 2,330 acres to Baldwin.

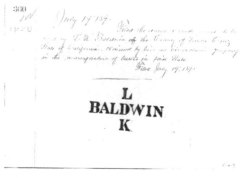

**L
BALDWIN
K**

The Baldwin Brand

Deloss D. Wilder
Churns up Ingenuity

The end of the partnership seemed to breathe new life into D.D. and Wilder Ranch. He moved his family from town onto the ranch land into Meder's old Gothic Revival style home near the old Castro and Bolcoff adobe structures. His butter making operations flourished expanding his herd to 300 under the new D.D. Wilder's Creamery name.

It was during the late 1880's, when he installed a Pelton Water Wheel on the property, that his ingenuity came to light. Wilder had a creek that ran through the property and about 1500 feet above the ranch, he dammed up the creek and had the diverted water fall some 216 feet to operate a number of pieces of machinery. When the water pressure was applied to the workshop and its series of belts and pulleys, it ran a buzz saw, a lathe, a drill, butter churn, cream separators, barley crushers, a coffee grinder, milk cooler, hay and feed cutters, emery wheel for sharpening blades and even a pumpkin and bone grinder.

With the help of his son Melvin, the Pelton wheel would operate a 110 volt dynamo bringing electricity to the ranch. It lit up large arches of light that woke the cows earlier, improving production. Some of the Pelton wheels are still in operation to this day and are turned on for visitors during park events.

D.D. Wilder Creamery - Santa Cruz

With D.D., the size of the barn doubled to keep up with his larger herd. As well, he built two granaries, a horse barn, a wagon shed and a workshop with bunkhouse for the workers above.

24

As the leader of the ranch, D.D. set the example as a hardworking and ethical man. Each time he would go into town to buy goods, he would take requests from his workers. In spite of having up to 29 ranch hands, D.D. never wrote down their requests nor did he forget any of them. As is stated in Francis', Beautiful Santa Cruz County (1896), "Deloss D. Wilder is the owner of the finest dairy farm in Santa Cruz County. Mr. Wilder is an old resident, is a man of fixed opinions, and whatever he sets out to do he always does."

Delos D Wilder

D.D.'s Two Sons, Melvin and Loss

D.D. and Miranda had two sons, Melvin and Deloss B who was nicknamed Loss. D.D. himself wanted very much to pass on the ranch to his two sons but there was one problem, neither wanted to become a dairy farmer. Loss enjoyed three things, hunting, fishing and gambling. Melvin on the other hand had higher aspirations, studying electrical engineering at Stanford University. Melvin had no desire to return once he finished his schooling but D.D. had one thing going for him, Melvin was sweet on a local girl named Leticia (Lettie) Anderson. To entice Melvin to stay and take over the ranch, he built a second Victorian home on the property and gave it to him in 1897. Melvin would marry Lettie, graciously accept the home his dad built for him as a wedding present and took over the ranch operations.

As stated earlier it was Melvin who built the 110 volt dynamo located in the machine shop using the Pelton water wheel his father built to power it. They became one of the first ranches in Santa Cruz County to have electricity.

Melvin was a strong Republican and had a picture of the then current President William McKinley put over the fireplace. It is clear from the many inventions he made to his home that he was a man who liked to bring innovation to his world. He had a log bin installed so that the wood stove could be heated by wood carried to the bin without tramping inside the house. As the women fueled the stove, they only had to open the bin from the porch.

He installed a switch to make opening the door to the kitchen possible without using one's hands. He installed lights in the closets to so that the closet lights would turn on when the door opened and turn off when the door was closed. He even had a battery powered switch to light up kerosene lanterns which were used to light up his bedroom after the generator had been shut down. At one point he tried converting the wood stove to a stove run by heating oil, but blew out the side of the stove due to the intensity of the heat produced.

Loss would live in the old farm-house until his 60's when he moved into town on Union Street. He married briefly to May Briody at the age of 38, but May died shortly after they were wed. While Melvin was ever the inventor, Loss was ever the sportsman who loved to hunt, fish and generally enjoy the outdoors.

Melvin After a Day's Hunt

Lettie Wilder, Melvin's Wife

Lettie must have been very proud the day she walked into her new home given to her by her father-in-law D.D. Wilder. Lettie and Melvin shared many happy years together on the ranch. She was, first and foremost, a mother to her two children Ethel and Deloss R (DR). She was heavyset, jovial and enjoyed sewing, cooking and generally performing the day to day comings and goings of Wilder Ranch.

When not being a homemaker, she would have friends and family over to the parlor for a game of cards. Poker games were her favorite and she was an exceptional player, able to not be bluffed by even the most steel-eyed player. Probably because of her weight she looked much older than Melvin (though she would out live him by 10 years). Folks would joke in a good natured way that Lettie must be Melvin's mother.

There is one story recounted by her grandson Dee. Dee and Billy were the sons of DR and lived in the upstairs portion of Melvin and Lettie's home. In the boy's room there was a long narrow hall and the boys would pour soap and water on the floor and get into sliding contests, seeing who could slide the farthest. On one occasion, they must have been doing sliding Olympics as they used so much water it seeped into Lettie's clothes closet downstairs, ruining all of her clothes. "Boy was she mad", remembers Dee.

Melvin and Lettie Standing Behind Their Prized Dahlias

Melvin's Daughter, Ethel Wilder

Melvin and Lettie had two children, Ethel and Deloss R. (nicknamed DR). Ethel was born three years prior to DR in 1898. In her teens she weighed 200 lbs and was 5'8". She would lose that weight and became known more for her flaming locks of red hair and rather delightful voice. Ethel would work alongside the men as a ranch hand. She wore men's style breeches which was quite unnatural in those days and even more noteworthy became the first woman truck driver in Santa Cruz. Ethel drove a Model T refitted into a one ton truck and helped load the 10 gallon (100 pound) cans of milk onto the truck. She would then make deliveries around town and was known to pick the cans up and "throw them over her back as well as any man could." Despite her tom-boyish nature, she was well-respected by both the town and other ranch hands, enjoying her individualistic personality and good nature.

Ethel and the Model T

Another Story about Kids and some Famous Items of Wilder

Another story about the children of Wilder involves two key items on the property. As you head towards the horse barn, look up to the top of it. You will see a traditional rooster and compass weathervane at the top spinning with the wind. To the left there is a large hose with a big pressure gauge on it.

The hose was built by D.D. from a design he picked up during his placer mining days and essentially produced the same hydraulic output used to hit hillsides with water to break up gold and dirt to be panned downstream. D.D. used the hydraulic hose he created to wash down the creamery.

Ethel and DR as Kids

The weathervane was also of importance as it was a gift given to D.D. and his wife from none other than L. K. Baldwin himself. Apparently the kids didn't realize the historical significance of either of these items and when the parents weren't home they would point the water hose at the weathervane and make it spin like a hurricane was happening. It's unknown how many times they actually performed this trick. It is known that after getting caught doing it, they never did it again.

DR Wilder, Ethel's Husband Goldie and the Tooth from Hell

DR was the second child of Melvin and Lettie and was born three years after Ethel. He also married Jean Williamson a few weeks before Ethel and her husband Goldie were married.

The life of DR contains an interesting story that involves Ethel's husband, Dr. Golden Bell Falconer or Goldie as people called him.

28

Goldie was a dentist in town and fairly prominent. He was characterized as "a tough cob with not much manners". In spite of this, Goldie and Ethel were good friends with comedians Laurel and Hardy and even travelled to Europe with them on vacation.

Having friends in Hollywood aside, Goldie liked to play around with a rather new device being used in dentistry, the x-ray machine. While common today, Goldie had one of the first x-ray machines in Santa Cruz. As it turns out, the machine and Goldie's knowledge in dentistry would save DR's life.

DR's problems began as paralysis in his extremities. With the inability to move his hands and feet, he required constant care and feeding. DR was taken to specialists at UC and Stanford but no one could determine what caused his malady. With no cure to be found and with his paralysis growing worse, the doctors eventually sent him home to die.

DR Minus a Tooth and Better For It

Goldie's sharp dentistry skills gave him an idea that potentially the ailment was caused by a problem with DR's teeth. Using his x-ray machine (and actually shocking DR in the process), Goldie was able to get a clean x-ray of DR's mouth. The x-ray plate revealed that DR's wisdom tooth had elongated and curved roots into the area of his 5th cranial nerve. The tooth was removed and that night DR was able to miraculously eat dinner with his family. Apparently the tooth is still in the Wilder family. Said family member Dee Wilder, "it's a vicious looking tooth".

Cow Pony Polo and the Ill Fate of Goldie

The Wilder Ranch played home to the Santa Cruz Polo Team during the 1920's. The field they used is where the Granite Rock Sand Plant now exists. Before the sand plant, the sand would wash down from the hills and flow out into a smooth playing area that would then invite grass to push up through the sand, creating a nice hard surface for polo.

The Santa Cruz Polo Team used cow ponies which were smaller horses trained for cattle herding. The cow ponies had a far superior means of maneuvering around the field than the larger horses, which led to defeating polo teams from Monterey and other clubs.

Goldie felt so confident with his cow pony that he used it during a rodeo event to rope a steer. The smaller horse lost its balance and knocked Goldie and his saddle off the horse. The pony landed square on Goldie's head giving him brain damage from which he never fully recovered. There is irony here. Goldie saved DR from a nerve injury close to the brain, only to suffer brain injury himself.

Zane Grey Was Here

Zane Gray Cutoff is one of the trails within Wilder and, yes, Zane Grey did work Wilder Ranch. "Work" may be a little too strong of a word for this writer of the American Frontier.

Zane worked as a herdsman on the ranch. The herdsman would wake each morning at 4am to gather the cattle. By 6am a bell would ring out over the hills and everyone would stop, come down and eat breakfast in the dining room of the old farmhouse. Throughout the day when the bell rang, it meant food was ready to be served. If you were late, you missed out as no one waited around for late comers. With breakfast over, the herdsman returned to the cows to start milking them.

After breakfast, the herdsman would go up into the hills and look for stray cattle. Zane Grey, who didn't really enjoy milking the cows took advantage of this. While bringing the cows in to be milked he would inadvertently leave a few cows behind that he just had to go back for. Ironically, Zane would bring the cows down from the hills just as milking time was over. After getting away with this tactic countless times, Zane was finally warned about his actions. On his last day, he was sent back out and came back with some 30 head of cattle! When he was asked where he had found all of them, he claimed they had all secluded themselves inside a cave up in the hills. Now the Wilders and the other herdsman knew quite well that the cave could hold at best two cows and everyone had a nice laugh about Zane's story of finding so many cattle hiding in such a small cavern. The Zane Grey Gulch leading to the cave is in honor of Zane and his "cave dwelling cow party".

When Rodeos Get Out of Hand

When the Wilder's switched from dairy farming to a beef cattle operation, it was natural that they developed a stronger interest in the rodeo as well. Rodeos were a huge craze at the Wilder Ranch during the 1930's and 1940's. The Wilders even ran a power line to the rodeo grounds to light up the arena for nighttime practices. The rodeo circuit started in Redbluff and included Carmel Valley and San Jose, making Wilder Ranch a natural midpoint for travelling cowboys hoping to make a buck in the rodeo. They would pay $10.00 to get in and could potentially win $100 through the bets made.

Before World War II Wilder Ranch entertained only nickel and dime bets for fun but after the war, the bets climbed with 40 cents becoming $40, which led to a more aggressive scene. The Wilder's feeling they would shortly become liable either for gambling or a fight gone wrong, closed the rodeo practices down altogether. I guess it goes to prove that if you send a cowboy off to war he will return a cowman.

All Parks Are Created From a Struggle

It has been said that there is not one state park in California that did not come about without some form of initial struggle. While this is likely debatable, Wilder Ranch State Park is an example of a park born out of the greed of a county and 1000 or so citizens who overcame that greed.

Melvin Wilder died in 1945 leaving the ranch in the hands of Deloss R (DR) Wilder. With Melvin there had already been a big change to Wilder Ranch. New sanitation regulations were enacted in 1937 which made it expensive to retrofit the existing equipment. Melvin made the call to turn the operation into a beef cattle ranch and sold all of his dairy cattle. When DR took over he found himself in charge of a successful beef cattle ranch. They would buy the beef cattle in Arizona for $35 per cow and calf and sell them for $200 per pair. As well, the family had been leasing the coastal flatlands to famers who grew artichokes and Brussels sprouts.

31

In 1957, while the Wilders were at the local drive-in movie theater, they watched as the screen stated "Wilders go home, your ranch is on fire". They returned to see the old creamery, now unused for 20 years, up in flames. The family used the hydraulic hose that D.D. himself had installed to wet down the adjoining buildings while they watched the creamery burn to the ground.

The creamery fire wasn't their only problem. The County of Santa Cruz saw a huge opportunity with the Wilder property. With it in the hands of developers they could push the town of Santa Cruz northward, potentially doubling its population from 30,000 to 60,000. With more residents came a larger tax base and thus more revenue for the county. In the late 1950's the land was rezoned from agricultural to residential which put a tremendous burden on the Wilders to create enough ranch income to pay the tax burden.

In 1959, DR was forced to lease 300 acres to the Granite Rock Cement Company in an effort to generate enough income to pay the taxes. By 1964, the Wilders began searching for a buyer and in July 1969 they sold their entire ranch to the Moroto Investment Co. Ltd, ending the Wilder family's ownership of the land.

For the county, everything was going as planned. UC Santa Cruz had been founded in 1965, which created an abundance of jobs and growth for the teachers and service employees. The Wilders had been effectively taxed off their own land and best of all, the sale went through to developers who could lead the way. Moroto Investment Co. Ltd. would become a subsidiary of Sussman Properties Ltd. and in 1972 they announced a large-scale development of the property. The development called for the creation of 9,000 to 10,000 housing units to be built over a period of 30 years. With this development, the City of Santa Cruz would more than double from its present size.

Fortunately for the land, when citizens heard of these plans, they reacted with outrage. Environmentalists had recently won a cause to keep a nuclear power plant from being installed near Davenport by Pacific Gas and Electric. They were quick to reform into Operation Wilder. The opposition didn't go without a fight and at one point tried to sue the leaders of Operation Wilder for unbelievable sum of $121 million. As it turns out this strategy may have worked to shut things down if the suit was for a reasonable amount. Given it was for a sum that would have taken Operation Wilder lifetimes to pay off, the leaders simply laughed at the lawsuit and by 1973 the community opposition won over the county's desires to expand. The California Department of Parks and Recreation purchased the land for $6 million in 1974. The State officially opened the park to the public in 1989 as a cultural and natural preserve, allowing visitors to appreciate the innovation and traditions of the Wilders and dairy their farming that was once practiced on these lands.

Sample Illustrations from Moroto Investment Company's plan "Wilder Ranch And Beaches" for "10,000 dwelling units in several distinct villages".

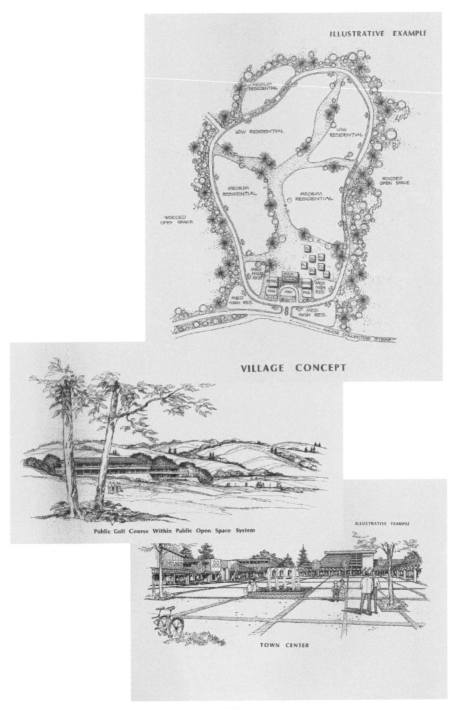

ILLUSTRATIVE EXAMPLE

VILLAGE CONCEPT

Public Golf Course Within Public Open Space System

ILLUSTRATIVE EXAMPLE

TOWN CENTER

Wilder Ranch Tour

Buildings of the Historic Wilder Ranch Complex
from an aerial photo, late 30's

A. Bolcoff Adobe (1830's)

B. Moses A. Meder House (1850's, remodeled later)

C. Wilder addition (Ca. 1912)

D. Dairy barn (left portion Ca. 1860's; right portion demolished 1950's)

E. Creamery (remodeled after 1892; burned 1957)

F. Granary (1880's)

G. Dairy heifer training shed

H. Dairy heifer feed shed

I. Bull shed for breed bulls

J. Springhouse

K. Manure storage shed

L. Storage barn; pig pen in rear

M. Dray horse (work horse) barn

N. Shop and bunkhouse (Ca. 1900)

O. Equipment and wagon house (Ca. 1879)

P. Horse barn (Ca. 1891-92)

Q. Melvin Wilder House (1896-97)

R. Garage (Ca. 1903)

S. Corn Crib

T. Old wooden tank

U. Slaughterhouse

V. Site of newest house (Ca. 1946-48)

W. Meder Creek (also: Arroyo de Matadero, Wilder Creek)

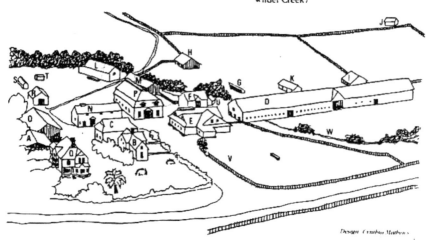

Design Cynthia Mathews

34

Arguably the most exciting part of the Wilder Ranch State Park is the ranch buildings themselves. Walking this portion of Wilder will transport the visitor back in time when the state was in its younger days. The buildings cover not only a wide range of time, from 1830-1912, but also represent a wide range of architectural styles. Each building has a unique connection in reflecting the history in which they were built.

A self-guided tour of Wilder Ranch historic structures will meet you at your pace. The slower you can take the structures in, the more they will tell. If you can allow yourself the proper pace, you can almost hear the clank, clank sounds of the blacksmith shop, the happy mooing of the dairy cows being milked, and the ringing of the dinner bell met with howlers and shout outs that it was time to eat.

Bolcoff Adobe

Bolcoff Adobe, Circa 1930's

This adobe structure was hand-built by the Bolcoff family around 1830. It is indeed built primarily of adobe made from soil within the Wilder property. First a sandstone foundation was constructed some 2 feet 8 inches high and the adobe walls were placed on top.

The roof is constructed of red tiles cast and fired in an oven to terracotta hardness. It is rumored that some of the tiles were actually removed by Bolcoff from the Mission Santa Cruz. Others were redone by the Wilders in the 1940's and other tiles still were added as part of Park renovation. The oldest tiles are found on the eastern slope.

The adobe building is one of four buildings believed to have been on the property. This remaining structure consists of two separate rooms with no interior door, which was common for this type of architecture. As well, there is evidence that suggests the northernmost room was an addition. Wooden post and lintel style entrances with wooden doors allow entrance into each room. The floor is made of compacted dirt.

While it is unknown with certainty what the structure was used for, theories do abound. Some say it was used as a detached kitchen, Indian living quarters or a cold storage room. One theory that is likely more popular myth than reality is the adobe was built in preparation for a "marriage feast and fandango" for the wedding of Maria del Los Angeles and Joseph Majors in 1839. There is little evidence to support this. The most likely theory is that the structure was used as a home.

Moses Meder Farmhouse

The farmhouse of Moses Meder is the first structure built by post-Hispanic ownership of the land. Moses had loaned money to Jose Bolcoff and Bolcoff was unable to repay which led to Moses acquiring the property. The original house was built in the 1850's and was remodeled twice, in 1904 and again in 1912. The home was built in the Gothic Revival style. It is thought that the original half was built by Meder himself and had cross gables with elaborate gothic detailing which is no longer present.

Moses Meder

The house has gone through a number of remodeling stints. There is evidence that the house actually stood on the east side of Meder Creek, (it is now on the west side of the creek). The house itself didn't move, but the creek did. Gothic detailing have been replaced by simpler gingerbread detailing. A rear wing was removed in 1904 and replaced with a kitchen, a bathroom and two bedrooms. A fire in 1906 then destroyed that new addition. Not to be deterred, the addition was rebuilt in 1912, which exists today and is the two-story square shaped section with double-hung windows.

The Meder House Showing Gothic Detailing. Deloss and Miranda Wilder Stand in Front

The house was extensively restored by the Friends of Santa Cruz State Parks. It is now furnished as a living museum. The kitchen was fully renovated as well as the cook room.

To listen for the bell, stand close to the rear door of this section. The original bell that would call the workers in for meals hangs there still.

Melvin Wilder Victorian

This magnificent example of Queen Anne Victorian architecture was built in 1896/1897 for D.D. Wilder's son, Melvin. Melvin had been studying electrical engineering at Stanford and while he was sweet on a local Santa Cruz girl, had a yearning to not follow in his father's footsteps at first. His dad built the house to help entice him to stay and gave it to him as a wedding present.

Early Photo of Wilder Victoria, Date Unknown

The design is in the style of the then locally famous architect E.L Van Cleeck. Amongst its features include turned gable ornaments, dormer windows (the windows that poke out of the roof), a semi-hipped roof and multiple gables. The first story is sided with shiplap siding while fishscale siding is used on the second story.

During the 1930's, the front and rear porches were enclosed with glass. In the 1940's, both the front and back parlors were remodeled into one large living area with hardwood oak floors.

In the interest of history, if you look out the front porch you will see two things, the road leading down from the parking lot and if you look closely, a hitching post. The post was used to tie up horses as folks travelled down this road, which at the time was the original Highway 1. Another interesting fact about the house is the western red cedar tree near the road. This large tree, beloved by young and old is over 100 years old. The Wilders planted it themselves from a seed packet they received in the mail. Red cedars typically grow vertically and get up to 200 feet tall. This cedar was planted in the front yard where it had all the room it wanted, so it grew outward instead. The tree remains a favorite with children who have been climbing its branches for a century.

Horse Barn

Horse Barn

The Wilder horse barn has stalls for 15 horses, is elegant in style and imposing at two stories. It was built in 1891/1892 and is constructed in shiplap siding with a hipped, broken-pitched roof (also known as Mansard style or French roof).

Inside, the stalls are arched and detailed in three-tone paint. The floor is the original bitumen (sticky oil sands), which was an early asphalt material used during this period and mined locally. The second story acted as a feed storage area. Box shafts connected to each stall allowed for direct feeding from the second floor to the stalls below. Note the paned glass windows on the second story front and sides.

Workshop and Bunkhouse

This two story building was built around 1900. Like the horse barn, it is made up of shiplap siding and is two stories in height. The second story contained the bunkhouse which was where the cowhands lived and slept.

There is an interesting story about the bunkhouse that occurred during Melvin's generation. Melvin's son, D. R., was planning on following in his father's footsteps and had been studying Creamery Management at UC Davis. Melvin and his brother Loss at this point were overseeing the business side of the ranch and left the entire supervision to the lead herdsman. One morning, the herdsman took a fatal spill down the stairs of the bunkhouse and broke his neck in the fall. Melvin and Loss were not able to run the dairy without the herdsman's knowledge and so they drove up to Davis to ask D.R. to return.

Workshop and Bunkouse

D.R. had no choice but to come back and help, in spite of also being offered a job by the Foremost Creamery. D.R.'s desire was to work for Foremost but familial duty called and D.R. would ultimately run both the dairy business and later the cattle ranching side of the ranch.

Cow Barn

The cow barn was built between 1860 and 1875, with the first half presumably built by Moses Meder. While both the Workshop and Horse Barn came later and were likely designed by the same individual, the cow barn has notable differences. It is constructed of whitewashed board and has a pitched roof of corrugated metal.

The second story, like that of the horse barn, was used to store hay and feed. Also upstairs there was a grinder for the feed plus a hopper that could move the grain from one end of the barn to other. As well, there were a series of pulleys and other devices that slid on rails to help move the heavy hay bails, which was dropped from the story above to the cows below.

Cow Barn

The cow barn was expanded in two phases and could accommodate a chorus of 200 contently mooing cows. The entire barn is built without nails. The older section features a mortise and tenon frame construction without continuous hand hewn beams. The second phase utilized butt-joint-toenail construction. This second phase proved to not be as long lasting and was torn down in the 1950's.

The cows were placed in stalls head-to-head and a hand drawn rail car was filled with the hay from above and rolled down the stalls to feed them. The rear of each stall had a cement floor with a trough in the center. Each day, a cowhand would wash down the cow excrement from the barn to Meder Creek. Makes one wonder what surfing was like near Wilder back then

Inside of the Cow Barn

Loading Hay Into the Cow Barn

Garage

The garage was built in 1903 and is built in vernacular constructed board and batten, which has been whitewashed and topped with a shake roof. The garage was built to house a real novelty back in 1901, a Knox automobile. Henry Ford's famous Model T, which brought the car

Garage

to the general public, was not introduced until 1908. Cars were new then and to a rancher the idea of not having to feed your transportation hay to achieve horsepower must have been a bold thought, indeed.

The Wilder's built the garage away from the other structures in case the car caught fire. Another Pelton wheel was installed here to charge the automotive batteries. At first the batteries were charged inside the garage until a couple exploded from overcharging. Thereafter, charging was done outside.

The Bungalow

This home, built around 1945/46 was built by D.R. Wilder for his family after his father, Melvin, died. Of the era, the home is made of a plain stucco wall for both the interior and exterior with a composition roof. This home, like many of the homes made immediately after World War II, were similar in architecture due to a high demand for housing coupled with a short-

Contemporary Residence

age of supplies. This is now the visitor and interpretation center for the park and houses a Friends of Santa Cruz State Parks Park Store. There is a small museum with detailed displays about the park's history and ecology.

Creamery

The creamery no longer stands but would have stood in the grassy area just to the left of the interpretive center. The creamery had not been used since 1936 and so when the Wilders were told it was on fire in 1957, they focused their collective energies to keeping the other buildings from burning. The Wilder's were at a local drive-in and saw a message on the movie screen saying something to the effect of "Wilder's, go home, your ranch is on fire".

The Creamery

At its peak, the creamery churned out over 300 pounds of the stuff every day. Given it takes 11 quarts of milk to make one pound of butter, this equates to 825 gallons of milk per day or over 300,000 gallons of milk produced every year on the ranch.

Various Outbuildings

There are several other outbuildings, including a springhouse, wagon and equipment shed, granary, heifer feed shed, bull shed, slaughter house, corn crib, draft horse barn, storage barn and manure storage shed. The granary among other buildings mentioned here, no longer stand.

Rush Hour at the Ranch

Park Maps

Wilder Ranch S.P. Map Key

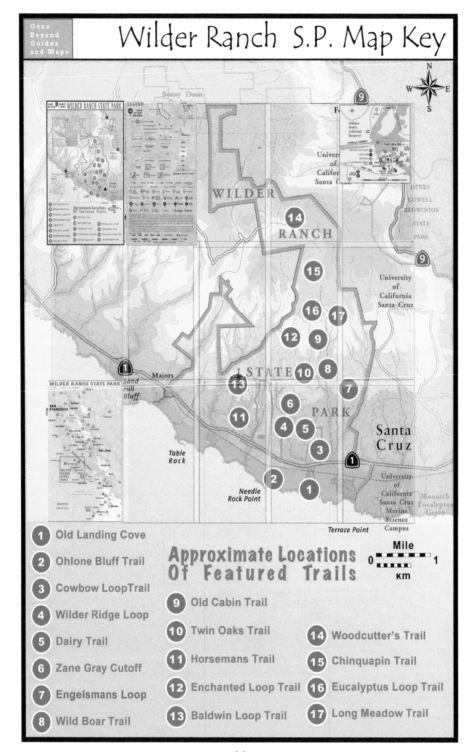

1. Old Landing Cove
2. Ohlone Bluff Trail
3. Cowbow LoopTrail
4. Wilder Ridge Loop
5. Dairy Trail
6. Zane Gray Cutoff
7. Engelsmans Loop
8. Wild Boar Trail

Approximate Locations Of Featured Trails

9. Old Cabin Trail
10. Twin Oaks Trail
11. Horsemans Trail
12. Enchanted Loop Trail
13. Baldwin Loop Trail

14. Woodcutter's Trail
15. Chinquapin Trail
16. Eucalyptus Loop Trail
17. Long Meadow Trail

Locality

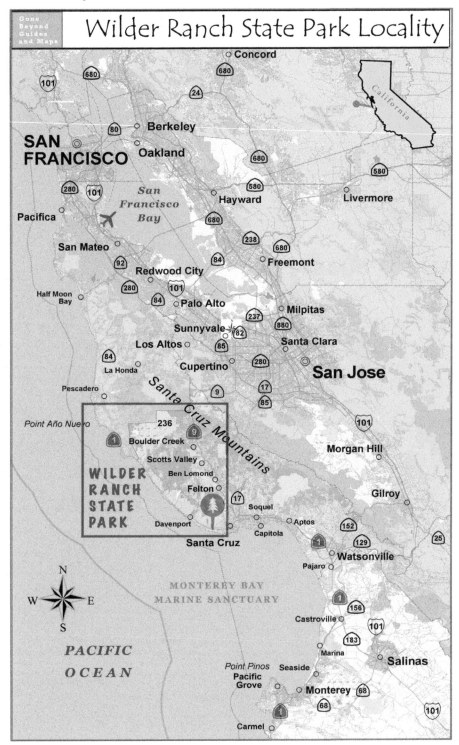

Legend

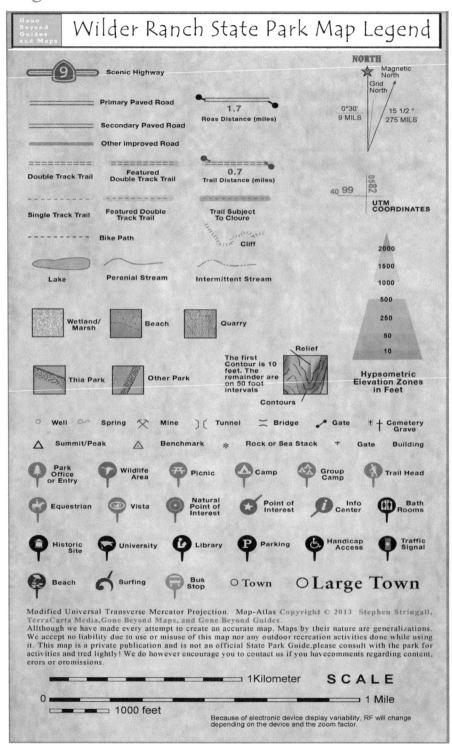

Wilder Ranch State Park Map Legend

Gone Beyond Guides and Maps

9   Scenic Highway

Primary Paved Road

Secondary Paved Road

Other improved Road

Double Track Trail

Featured Double Track Trail

Single Track Trail

Featured Double Track Trail

Bike Path

Lake

Perenial Stream

Intermittent Stream

1.7
Roas Distance (miles)

0.7
Trail Distance (miles)

Trail Subject To Cloure

Cliff

NORTH

Magnetic North

Grid North

0°30'
9 MILS

15 1/2 °
275 MILS

40 99 0582

UTM COORDINATES

2000
1500
1000
500
250
50
10

Wetland/ Marsh   Beach   Quarry

Thia Park   Other Park

Relief

The first Contour is 10 feet. The remainder are on 50 foot intervals

Contours

Hypsometric Elevation Zones in Feet

○ Well   ⌒ Spring   ⚒ Mine   )(Tunnel   ≃ Bridge   ● Gate   † † Cemetery Grave

△ Summit/Peak   ⟁ Benchmark   ✳ Rock or Sea Stack   ÷ Gate   Building

Park Office or Entry   Wildlife Area   Picnic   Camp   Group Camp   Trail Head

Equestrian   Vista   Natural Point of Interest   Point of Interest   Info Center   Bath Rooms

Historic Site   University   Library   Parking   Handicap Access   Traffic Signal

Beach   Surfing   Bus Stop   ○ Town   ○ Large Town

1 Kilometer   **SCALE**

0   1 Mile

1000 feet

Because of electronic device display variability, RF will change depending on the device and the zoom factor.

Topograhpic Maps

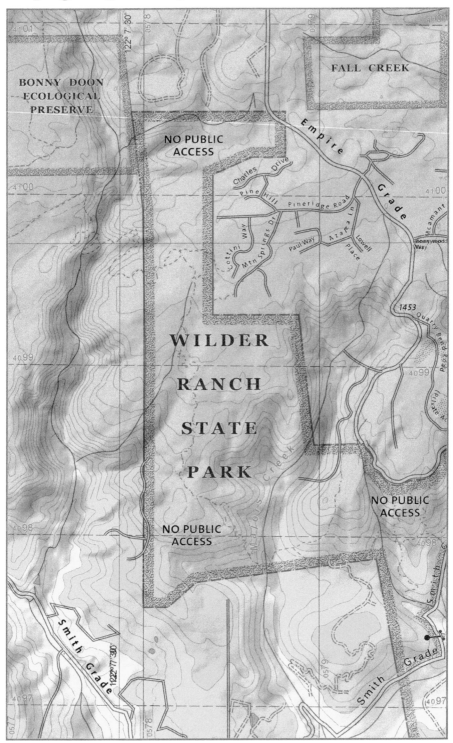

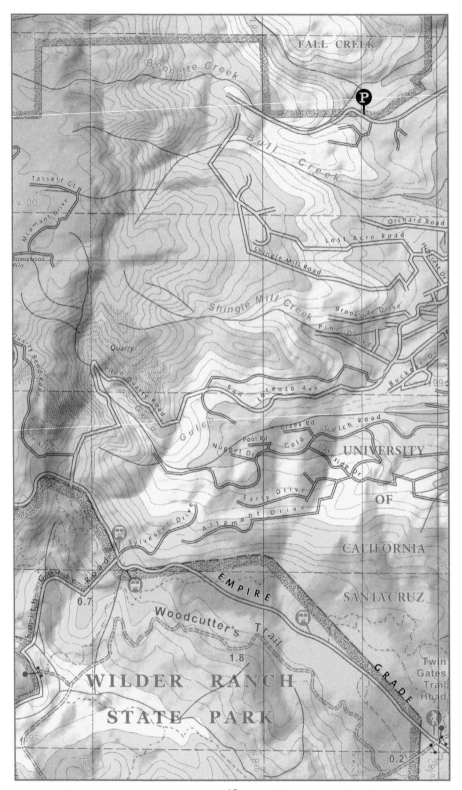

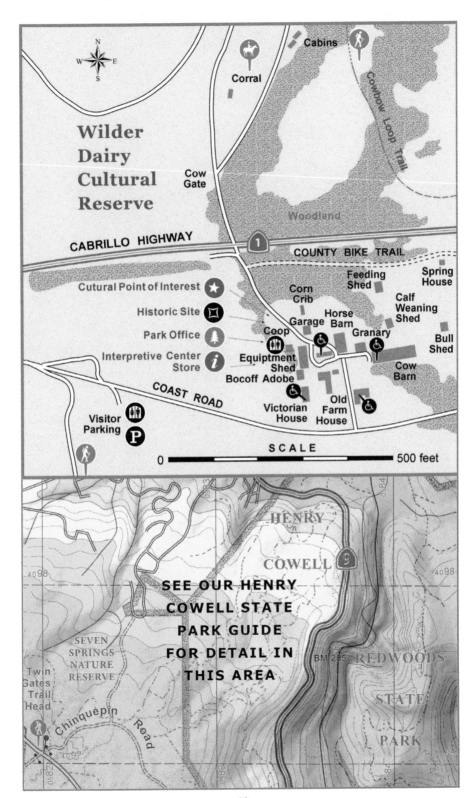

Wilder
Dairy
Cultural
Reserve

CABRILLO HIGHWAY

Cow
Gate

Cabins

Corral

Woodland

Cowbow Loop Trail

COUNTY BIKE TRAIL

Cutural Point of Interest

Historic Site

Park Office

Interpretive Center
Store

Corn
Crib

Feeding
Shed

Spring
House

Calf
Weaning
Shed

Horse
Barn

Garage

Granary

Bull
Shed

Coop

Equiptment
Shed

Bocoff Adobe

Cow
Barn

COAST ROAD

Victorian
House

Old
Farm
House

Visitor
Parking

P

SCALE

0   500 feet

HENRY

COWELL

SEE OUR HENRY

COWELL STATE

PARK GUIDE

FOR DETAIL IN

THIS AREA

SEVEN
SPRINGS
NATURE
RESERVE

Twin
Gates
Trail
Head

BM 285

REDWOODS

STATE

PARK

Chinquepin   Road

4098

4098

4097

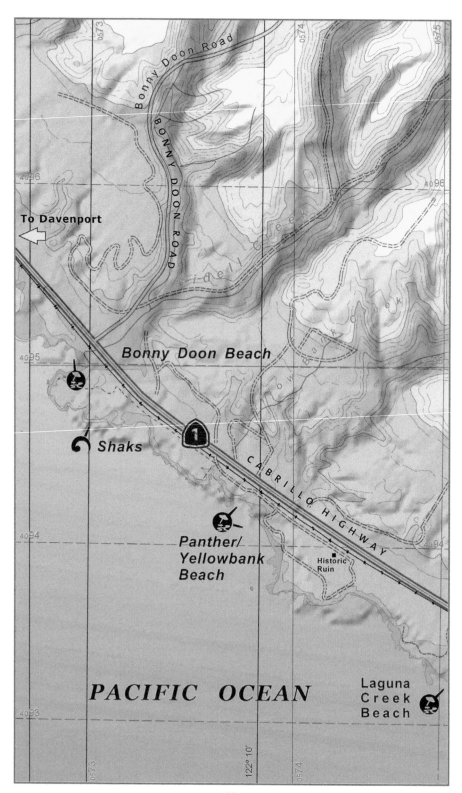

To Davenport

Bonny Doon Road

BONNY DOON ROAD

Bonny Doon Beach

Shaks

CABRILLO HIGHWAY

Panther/
Yellowbank
Beach

Historic
Ruin

PACIFIC OCEAN

Laguna
Creek
Beach

122° 10'

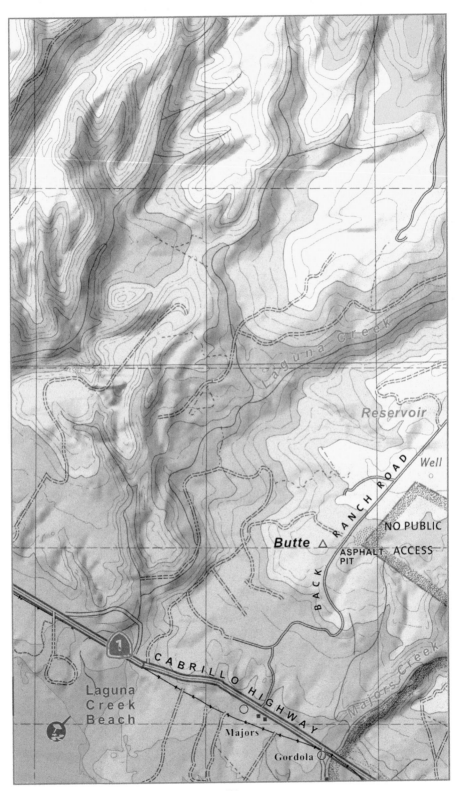

Laguna Creek

Reservoir

Well

BACK RANCH ROAD

NO PUBLIC

Butte △

ASPHALT ACCESS
PIT

CABRILLO HIGHWAY

Laguna
Creek
Beach

Majors

Gordola

Majors Creek

51

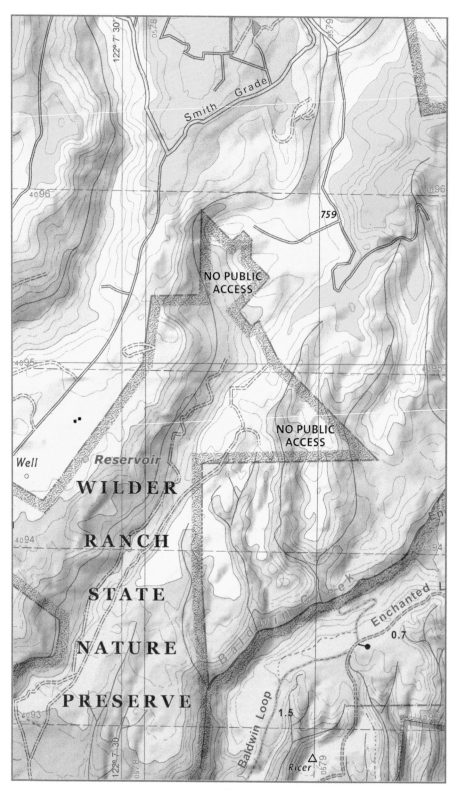

NO PUBLIC
ACCESS

759

NO PUBLIC
ACCESS

Smith Grade

Well

Reservoir

WILDER

RANCH

STATE

NATURE

PRESERVE

Baldwin Creek

Enchanted L

0.7

Baldwin Loop

1.5

Ricer

122° 7′ 30″

4096

4095

4094

4093

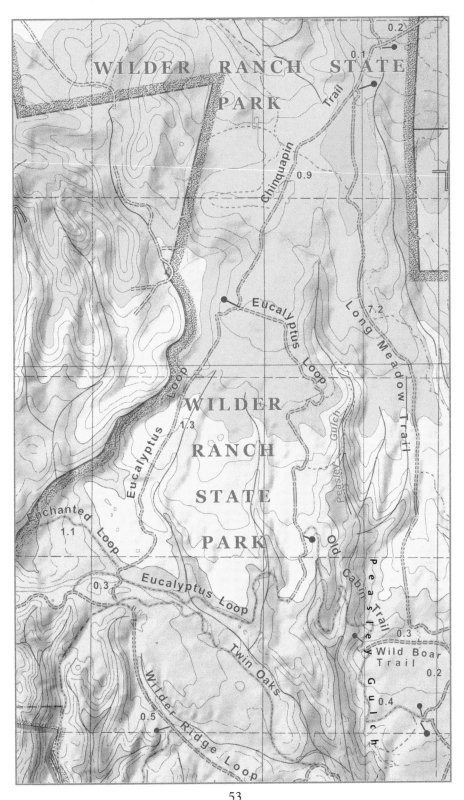

WILDER RANCH STATE PARK

WILDER RANCH STATE PARK

Chinquapin Trail

0.2

0.1

0.9

Eucalyptus Loop

Long Meadow Trail

7.2

1.3

Eucalyptus Loop

Peasley Gulch

Enchanted Loop

1.1

0.3

Eucalyptus Loop

Old Cabin Trail

Peasley Gulch

Peas Trail

0.3

Wild Boar Trail

0.2

0.4

Twin Oaks

Wilder Ridge Loop

0.5

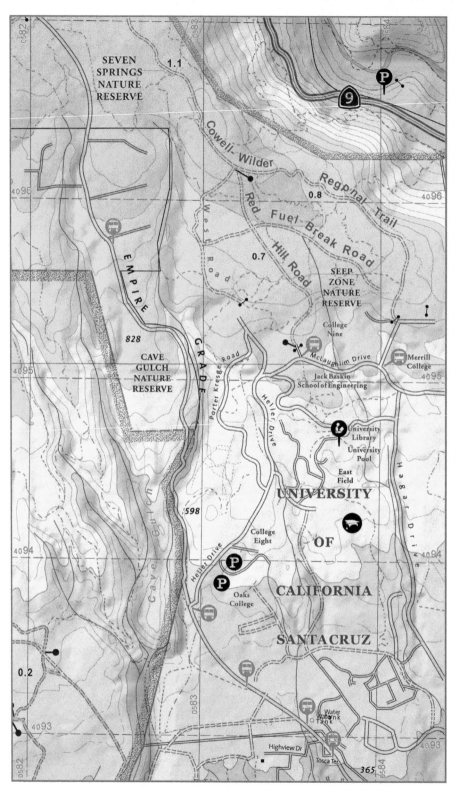

SEVEN
SPRINGS
NATURE
RESERVE

1.1

9

P

Cowell-Wilder

Regional Trail

0.8

Red Fuel Break Road

West Road

0.7

Hill Road

SEEP
ZONE
NATURE
RESERVE

College
Nine

EMPIRE

828

GRADE

CAVE
GULCH
NATURE
RESERVE

Porter Kresge Road

McLaughlin Drive

Merrill
College

Jack Baskin
School of Engineering

Heller Drive

University
Library

University
Pool

East
Field

UNIVERSITY

598

Cave Gulch

Heller Drive

College
Eight

OF

Hagar Drive

CALIFORNIA

P

P

Oaks
College

SANTA CRUZ

0.2

Water
Tank

Highview Dr

Tosca Ter

365

54

Laguna
Creek
Beach

Sand Hill Bluff

Gordola

Reservoir

Red White
and Blue
Beach

Table Rock

5 Mile

Monterey Bay

PACIFIC OCEAN

122°57'30"

122°57'30"

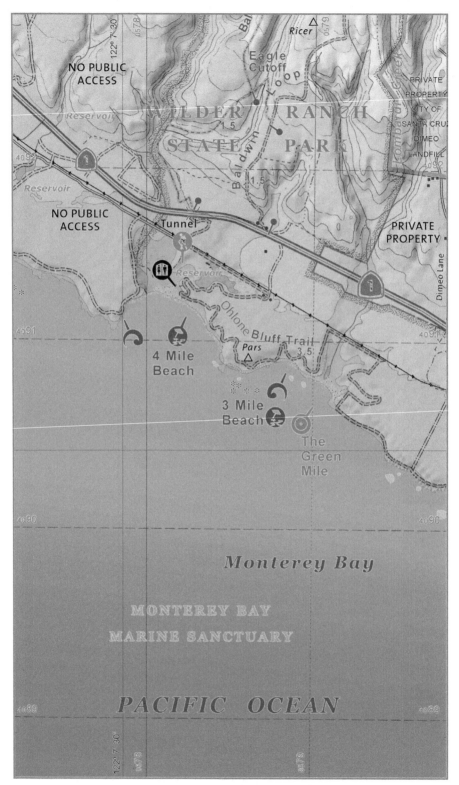

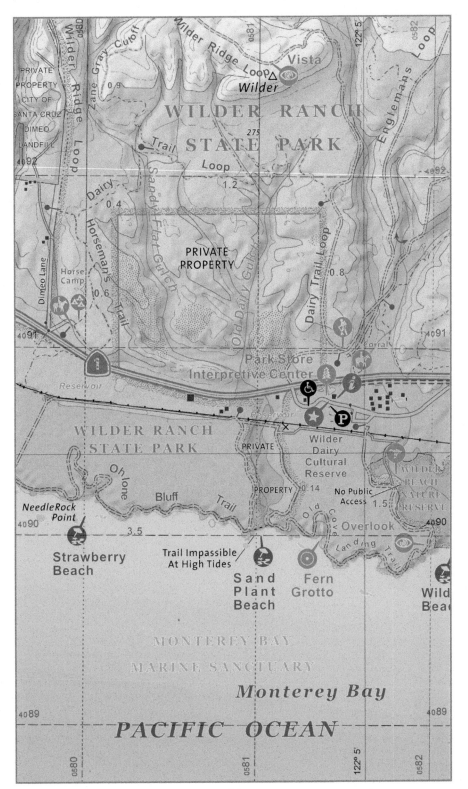

Trails

There are a total of 17 formally recognized trails in Wilder, comprising a full 34 miles of access by bike, foot or horse. The trails cover coastal bluffs, oak chaparral, and mixed evergreen forests. There are many to choose from and many of the park's trails interconnect, creating an endless variety of adventures.

Old Landing Cove Trail

Difficulty: Easy

Distance: 2.49 miles

Duration: 1-3 hours

Elevation Gain/Loss: +65 feet/-62 feet

Best For: Families, strolls, quiet coastal reflection, inaugural beach cruiser run

This old ranch road is an easy mostly level walk, allowing the viewer to relax and take in the many sights as the trail rambles to an old schooner landing. Along the way you will see a pristine natural preserve giving great examples of north coast bluffs, waterfowl and rugged north coast scenery. Depend on the season; you may even spot passing whales on their annual migrations. This trail connects into the Ohlone Bluff Trail where you can extend your hike into a 10 mile loop.

Directly off the main parking lot adjacent to the restrooms is the trailhead for the Old Landing Cove Trail. Cross the train tracks and head towards the coast. On your left is Wilder Beach, now a natural preserve protecting the Snowy Plover. Amazingly, prior to the 1994 restoration, this beach was an agricultural field. On your right are some 900 acres devoted to the beloved Brussels sprout.

Making your way to the bluff of the coast's edge you will soon come to Old Landing Cove. Between the 1850 - 1890's, schooners navigated close to shore in this little cove to pick up lime and lumber. With binoculars, one can spot iron rings struck into the cliff, which once supported landing chutes for the products. At low tide, harbor seals can be seen sunning themselves just offshore.

If you head down to the cove itself, look for a fern filled sea cave. The sword and braken ferns are watered from an underground spring. The cave doesn't go too far back, so no flashlights are needed, though your crouching abilities may be tested.

The trail continues another half mile along the bluffs before heading inland. This beach, currently called Sand Plant Beach due to it being downstream to a sand refinery, was once referred to as Smuggler's Beach. The beach today is quite relaxing and worth a stop. You can either return the way you came, take the railroad tracks back or continue on to the Ohlone Bluff Trail.

Wilder Once Had Its Own Natural Bridge

Ohlone Bluff Trail

Difficulty: Moderately Easy (flat but some miles)

Distance: 10.5 miles as stated

Duration: 3-5 hours

Elevation Gain/Loss: +60 feet/- 62 feet

Best For: folks looking for a not too strenuous hike/bike combined with multiple secluded beach opportunities

Most people pick up this trail from the Old Landing Cove Trail but you can also pick it up from Highway 1 at Four Mile Beach. While there is ample parking at the main parking lot, it does come with a $10 park fee. The Four Mile Beach parking lot is free, but only holds 20 cars and is popular with out of town surfers.

The trail makes for an excellent coastal hike, meandering along coastal bluffs on an old ranch road to a number of relatively secluded beaches. Plenty of wildlife viewing opportunities including whale watching in season can be found.

If you connect up from the Old Landing Cove Trail, simply continue following the obvious trail markings up the coast. If you decide to start at the Four Mile Beach, parking will be on the coastal side about 0.2 miles north of 3800 Highway 1. You won't see a sign indicating you found the Four Mile Beach, but it is fairly evident due to the number of parked cars.

Depending on which way you go, you will hit Four Mile Beach, Three Mile Beach, (both named for their distance from Santa Cruz), Strawberry Beach, Sand Plant Beach and Fern Grotto. All of these are great beaches to relax and pour sand in your navel.

There are a few obvious spots where you can loop back to where you started along the railroad tracks. This gives the hiker some opportunities to cut out or extend their hike with little extra planning.

Cowboy Loop Trail

Difficulty: easy, some small creek crossings

Distance: 1.5 miles

Duration: 1-2 hours

Elevation Gain/Loss: +253 feet/-259 feet

Best For: mountain bikers looking for a warm up, hikers who like to say "Giddy Up!" at the start of trail heads.

Portions of this part of the park are within a couple thousand feet from the Moore Creek Preserve which has been set aside by the City of Santa Cruz to protect a number of special status species that require protection, including the California red-legged frog, the southwestern pond turtle, and the San Francisco popcorn flower. With protection comes preservation, so it's a great trail to see undisturbed coastal California from a distance. The preserve is named after Eli Moore, a rancher in the 1840's.

You can access the Cowboy Loop Trail by going through the tunnel near the ranch and past the corrals to the wooden bridge crossing Wilder Creek. Take an immediate left after the bridge, crossing the small creek.

The trail itself is underused by hikers and bikers but is often used by horses accessing nearby Jade Ranch. Going clockwise on the loop, you start in the shade of some trees before climbing steeply for a short distance. With the climb surmounted, the trail crosses an open meadow with the ocean in the distance. Continue the loop to meet back to where you started. Watch out for endo causing holes if you are biking this loop.

Wilder Ridge Loop Trail

Difficulty: Moderate

Distance: 7.7 -10.5 miles

Duration: 3 – 6 hours

Elevation Gain/Loss: +600 feet/-602 feet

Best For: Mountain bikers, equestrian riders and hikers

Gently sloping grassy meadows, the ocean in the distance and easy to get to, the Wilder Ridge Loop Trail, aka the "Dairy Trail" is a popular one for both mountain bikers and hikers.

Start on the Englesmann Trail from the tunnel near Wilder Ranch until you get past the corrals on your left. From here you will climb slowly and steadily. With each step you will see the ocean spread out before you with Wilder Beach down towards your left. Wilder Beach is now a nature preserve for the Snowy Plover and native plants and is a model example of coastal restoration.

As you come to the top of the hill you will find a nice wide path which will lead you to a junction that marks the beginning of the loop. Look for it just past the pond where you will see a sign. Travelling clockwise take the left fork which will put you on an old "dairy" trail. This left fork to Zane Gray Cutoff is shown on some maps as The Dairy Trail. Looking up and to your right you will see Wilder Ridge, which you will be taking back home.

The trail will cross the Old Dairy Gulch and the Sandy Flat Gulch before hitting the marked trail sign for the Zane Gray Cutoff at 1.2 miles. Here you have two choices; shorter hike or longer hike which will add 3 miles to your hike.

• For shorter, you can take the Zane Gray Cutoff for about a mile will connect you back to the ranch road that makes up the Wilder Ridge. There are two climbs along this part, the second being the longest, and winding along the far edge of the bluff.

• For a longer climb, keep travelling on the Wilder Ridge Loop Trail for about 2 miles, passing first the Horseman's Trail and towards the top of the ridge, the Enchanted Loop Trail where you will want to stay to your right.

Once at the top, you are welcomed with views of the Pacific Coast stretching as far south as Monterey Bay. On a spring day, the green meadows and the unparalleled view are little changed from what Wilder himself would have seen while working his land.

Keep right to complete the journey back down or go left into the deeper sections of Wilder. The journey back give consistently amazing ocean views, but the trip can be breezy, so bring a windbreaker. There is a picnic table along the ridge nicknamed "The Lookout", which is a wonderful place to take it all in one last time. Continue the gentle decent past the Twin Oaks trail back to the Englesmann Trail and the start of your journey.

Dairy Trail

See the Wilder Ridge Loop Trail. This is called out as part of the Wilder Ranch Loop Trail, look there for additional details. Start on the Englesmann Trail from the tunnel near Wilder Ranch, connect with Wilder Ranch Loop Trail, and then see a fork to the left just after the pond. Taking the fork puts you on the Dairy Trail, passing Old Dairy Gulch and Sandy Flat Gulch. Gray foxes (Urocyon cinereoargenteus) have been seen here.

Zane Gray Cutoff

Difficulty: Moderate

Distance: 0.96 mile

Duration: 30 minutes

Elevation Gain/Loss: +47 feet/-325 feet

Best For: adding variety to your hike

The Zane Gray Cutoff was named after famed American author Zane Grey. His last name actually did start out as Gray but his family changed the spelling of their name to Grey early in life. As you ponder taking this cutoff, bring along a copy of Riders of the Purple Sage with you, which was Zane's bestselling book back in 1912.

The Zane Gray Cutoff is a practical trail. It is a trail of opportunities and variety. You can use it to cut 3 miles off the Wilder Ridge Loop Trail. You can combine it with the Wilder Ridge Loop and the Twin Oaks Trail to make a figure eight loop. You can get really fancy and do a triple loop; I'll leave that to you to figure out.

There are two climbs along this trail, the second being the longest and winding along the far edge of the bluff.

Engelsmans Loop Trail

Difficulty: Moderate

Distance: 3.08 mile

Duration: 3-5 hours

Elevation Gain/Loss: +476 feet/-480 feet

Best For: getting a great taste of what everyone's talking about, starting point for longer journeys.

Wilder Ranch sits in the rarified saddle of being called out as one of the top mountain biking destinations. Perhaps it's because of the beauty, the ocean spreading out as you climb; perhaps it's simply the fact of riding a 21st century mountain bike on land that is little changed since the 1800's. Whatever the reason for Wilder's accolades, there is one trail that offers a great example of this praise, Engelsmans Loop Trail. You can take it up and back as is described here or use it as an entry point to longer journeys, connecting to the Eucalyptus Loop and Long Meadow Trail. There are several options to connect with other trails from this one. Expect stunning views of the ocean both up and back. Expect to hear the sound of grass rustling with the wind as it travels up the hillside. Expect to hear the melody of crickets replace the normal day to day thoughts as you realize this is going to be a good day.

This trail is named after Led Engelsman, who was a Wilder foreman and champion rodeo rider during the 1930's and 1940's when the ranch was turned over to raising beef cattle. Engelsmans Loop recently received a nice face lift on the northern side, cutting off the old trail that was causing erosion issues. Go through the tunnel from the Ranch and head to the end of the corral, crossing a bridge and bypassing the first of two main forks you will see. The fork for Engelsmans is clearly marked and either route will start you on this loop, we will take the northern one to the left and describe a clockwise route. Note the Cowboy Loop Trail as the one that makes a sharp right rather than going straight. A left climb is slightly steeper to the gentler sloped right fork, giving you more chances to take a break and look out over the view.

The trail winds continuously up to an open grassy hillside before ducking into a more wooded area connecting with the 4 way crossroads of Englesmans Loop, Long Meadow Trail and Wild Boar Trail. Up on your right you will see an old ranch fence, which marked the boundary of Samuel Adams and Wilder's property and is estimated to be over 100 years old.

There is a fairly well preserved lime kiln site just past this crossroad on Long Meadow Trail. See the section on lime kilns for additional detail on everything you wanted to know about the lime industry in Santa Cruz, it's a story that will stick with you.

Connecting back and continuing clockwise on Englemans's Loop will take you past the old ranch fence and ultimately back to where you started. The gentle slope is easy on the limbs coming down allowing you to take in the views of Monterey Bay on a clear day.

Wild Boar Trail

Difficulty: Moderate

Distance: 0.3 mile

Duration: 30 minutes to 1 hour

Elevation Gain/Loss: + 25 feet/-20 feet

Best For: getting from Engelsmann Loop Trail to Old Cabin Trail, and Eucalyptus Loop Trail.

Wild Boar is not listed on the park brochure but is not completely unloved, as it is on the trail markers. Short and sweet, you can pick up the Wild Boar Trail at the 4 way crossroads of Englesmann Loop, Long Meadow Trail and Wild Boar Trail.

It connects one to the Old Cabin Trail, which in turn gets you to the Eucalyptus Loop Trail. When connecting to Wild Boar from Englesmann Loop, don't confuse it with the beginning of Old Cabin Trail, which is a single track trail. Wild Boar is farther on, is at the crossroads and is a well-marked, well-travelled ranch road. The trail names get a little confusing depending on which map you have, so remember, Old Cabin; single track, Wild Boar; ranch road.

Old Cabin Trail

Difficulty: Moderate

Distance: 0.96 mile

Duration: 30 minutes to 1 hour

Elevation Gain/Loss: +149 feet/-269 feet

Best For: some great single track mountain biking and hiking.

The Old Cabin Trail connects the former ranch road Englesman Loop Trail to another former ranch road the Eucalyptus Loop Trail. While the trail itself is short, it is nicely wooded, with a carpet of ferns beneath a canopy of trees. It can get a little hilly in some places, with brush on either side. This is a nice single track trail overall.

Twin Oaks Trail

Difficulty: Moderate

Distance: 1.07 mile

Duration: 30 minutes to 1 hour

Elevation Gain/Loss: +221 feet/-62 feet

Best For: getting in an extra loop in the late afternoon.

The Twin Oaks Trail is a wonderful single track, with bridges, short climbs and the seclusion of the forest canopy alternating to open meadows. The trail itself connects from Wilder Loop Trail back to the Wilder Loop Trail further along. Either way, connect to this trail from the well-marked signs leading the way. You will not be disappointed. Where are the twin oaks you say? Pretty much anyone's guess at this point, though starting from the eastern entrance to the trail and going about a quarter mile to your first large meadow will showcase as likely a pair of large oaks as any on your right.

Horsemans Trail

Difficulty: Moderate

Distance: 0.6 mile

Duration: 30 minutes to 1 hour

Elevation Gain/Loss: +128 feet/-4 feet

Best For: Getting from Ohlone Bluff Trail to Wilder Ridge Trail.

For mountain bikers, this trail doesn't have much to offer but does offer a nice connection point if you are starting a trek, either by bike or foot from the bluff to inland reaches via Wilder Ridge Loop. The Horseman's Trail is aptly named as it houses the Wilder horse camping area.

If you do want to camp at the horse camp, after making the necessary arrangements with the park, head north on Highway 1 for about 3 miles past the city limits of Santa Cruz until you see Dimeo Lane. This is easy to spot as it is also the turn off for the city landfill. Turn right here where you will see a locked gate. There is good room here to get the trailer and truck in while you unlock the gate. Once through, follow the paved road steeply into the camping area. For the gate code, call 831-423-9403.

For hikers and bikers, you can access the trail from the Ohlone Bluff Trail by taking the obvious cut back to the highway a little north of Strawberry Beach. Take the road through the tunnel under Highway 1 to Dimeo Lane and the Horseman's Trail.

Enchanted Loop Trail

Difficulty: Moderately strenuous, technical

Distance: 1.5 mile

Duration: 30 minutes to 1 hour

Elevation Gain/Loss: +304 feet/-304 feet

Best For: Bikers looking to say, "Wow, I almost ate it! That was amazing!"

This trail is a favorite amongst the mountain bike community. Most bike it clockwise to give a wonderful combination of steep technical descent followed by a long rather strenuous climb out. Lots of roots combined with a steep descent make this fairly technical at the beginning of the loop. After a quarter mile, you will be past the rooty technical bits, on to a couple of switchbacks before landing in quaint little valley. Enjoy your respite before hitting an exhausting climb back out.

You get to this trail by starting at the Wilder Ridge Loop, Baldwin Loop or Eucalyptus Loop Trails.

Baldwin Loop Trail

Difficulty: Moderately strenuous, technical

Distance: 3.04 miles

Duration: 2-4 hours

Elevation Gain/Loss: + 589 feet/-584 feet

Best For: A longer but scenic all in one loop or the lower half of a nice figure 8 loop hike.

The eastern section of the Baldwin Loop Trail is cited as Sea Ridge Trail on some maps, however on the park map, it's all culled together as one trail. The Baldwin Loop Trail offers wide open views of the Pacific Ocean as you travel through tranquil grasslands.  You can just do Baldwin Loop Trail itself or connect to the Enchanted which is the yin to Baldwin's yang (technical vs. tranquil).

The trail's namesake comes from Wilder's partner, Levi K. Baldwin. You can either access the Baldwin Loop from above from the Twin Oaks Trail or from Wilder Ridge which will connect you to the Enchanted Loop Trail and finally to the well marked Baldwin Loop. From below, take Ohlone Bluff Trail past the 4 Mile Beach parking lot access to an often overgrown, hard to find trail that leads to Highway 1. Once you cross the highway, you will follow an old wooden fence briefly. Right after the fence, take a fork to your right to start the Baldwin Loop Trail counterclockwise. This early section can often get overgrown with stinging nettle and thorny stuff, but once you are past this, it opens up nicely for the rest of the ride.

Counterclockwise and going uphill, you will find yourself on the old ranch road that Baldwin took. While you can connect to the Enchanted Loop Trail, if you do decide to head back to Highway 1 via Baldwin Loop, you will find this portion has wide open views of the ocean and a very narrow single track to descend on. As you reach the highway, you meet up with similar not so neighborly vegetation that you met coming up.

Woodcutter's Trail

Difficulty: Moderate

Distance: 1.8 miles

Duration: 1-3 hours

Elevation Gain/Loss: +435 feet/ -412 feet

Best For: Hot days, getting a wooded hike, seeing what the most inland trail in the park is like.

The Woodcutter's Trail, if accessed from the Ohlone Bluff Trail will have taken you from a serene coastal venture, up through breezy meadows and the nutty smells of oak chaparral into the outer regions of the parks evergreens and redwoods. The Wood-cutter's Trail is the farthest trail in from the shore, though it can be accessed via the Smith or Empire Grade Roads easily. This trail is almost totally wooded, with second growth Redwoods, laurels, Madrones, and Douglas Firs, offering a vastly different experience than many of the other trails. There are also a couple of fun creek crossings. The portion of the park is part of a recent addition to Wilder through the purchase of the Gray Whale Ranch, which added some 2300 acres in 1996. As this area does tend to get a lot of rain in the winter, the trail can get washed out from time to time, so inquire before you go.

Accessing is easy enough from the east via the Empire Grade Road as at what is dubbed by locals as Twin Gates, a four way crossing consisting of Chinquapin Trail and Empire Grade. Parking at the gates is not allowed, so plan to park and walk a bit to get to the trail. From Chinquapin Trail, head west (away from the UC Santa Cruz portion of Chinquapin) and you will soon pick up Woodcutter's. Heading west for 1.8 miles will take you to the trails end where it dumps into Smith Grade Road. Neither Smith nor Empire offer easy access parking.

Alternately, if coming from the visitor's center the trail is found via Long Meadow or Chinquapin Trails.

Chinquapin Trail

Difficulty: Moderately Easy

Distance: 1.4 miles

Duration: 1-3 hours

Elevation Gain/Loss: +427 feet/-414 feet

Best For: The trail for getting you from UC Santa Cruz to Wilder Ranch State Park.

The irony in writing a trail guide is if you are local, you already know about the Chinquapin trail. If you are a UC Santa Cruz college student, let's face it, this trail is one of the reasons you came here. You can go from cramming for a test to unwinding on a wooded trail in minutes. So students, let's just say we wrote this to help out your parents when they come for a visit.

Chinquapin Trail gets the traveler from the Empire Grade road at what is locally referred to as the "Twin Gates" to the Eucalyptus Loop Trail and Long Meadow Trail. This trail is well used and definitely has appeal. Even if you are just passing through on Empire Grade, the trail, with its tranquil grassy meadows on either side, just seems to beckon the driver to get out and get lost on this trail. That being said, the lack of parking may cause you to keep driving. If you do access the trail from Empire Grade, be prepared to park above or below the Twin Gates and walk to the trail. As stated earlier, Chinquapin is part of the Gray Whale Ranch portion of Wilder Ranch State Park.

Eucalyptus Loop Trail

Difficulty: Moderately Easy

Distance: 3.3 miles

Duration: 2-4 hours

Elevation Gain/Loss: +438 feet/-411 feet

Best For: The trail for getting you from UC Santa Cruz to Wilder Ranch State Park.

Used as either a loop or an extension to other trails, Eucalyptus Loop Trail offers fairly easy ranch road for most of the journey with a bit of single track to loop the two roads together.

Many pick up the Eucalyptus Loop Trail from Old Cabin Trail, which is a nice wooded single track in its own right. You can also pick up the Eucalyptus Loop Trail from the west via the Enchanted Loop Trail or from the north via the Chinquapin Trail.

The Eucalyptus Loop is one of the gems of Wilder, traversing through wooded canopies draped with laurel and ferns on the forest floor before opening up to rolling hills of grass and the sounds of field insects basking in the sun. In the near distance, the blue of the Pacific fades into a distant fog bank or extends to the horizon, giving views of Monterey Bay.

If you do find yourself on a day when Monterey is visible, you are looking at the former state capital while under Mexico's control until 1846. By the time Wilder arrived in 1853, California was newly a part of the United States, with Vallejo and Benicia both sharing the title of State Capital before it finally landed in Sacramento.

Long Meadow Trail

Difficulty: Moderate

Distance: 2.37 miles

Duration: 1-3 hours

Elevation Gain/Loss: +606 feet/-32 feet

Best For: Resetting.

If you are looking for a hike that is a bit of a work out on the way up, but is full of rambling views and easy on the knees going down, find your way to the top of Long Meadow Trail and take its carefree route. In the late afternoon, the sun will cast a warm glow on a big sky California meadow banded by green forests and the Pacific Ocean's comfortable blue color in the distance. Your shadows will look larger than life as you stroll down a wide gently sloping trail back towards home.

You can access the trail from the northern top of the park via Chinquapin Trail or from the park's Interpretive Center via Engelsmans Loop or Old Cabin Trail. There is a fairly well preserved lime kiln site just past this crossroad on Long Meadow Trail. The Lime Kilns were first operated by Samuel Adams who later sold out to Henry Cowell (of Henry Cowell State Park fame.)

Flora

The vegetation within Wilder Ranch State Park is surprisingly diverse for an area encompassing only 7,000 acres. For the California Park System to accurately identify just the vegetation types, they had to define 24 separate communities. In order to make this a little simpler, the docents at Wilder have grouped the flora of the park into a manageable 6 plant communities.

Plant communities are simply areas where vegetation tends to grow. Plants that are often found in wetlands typically don't do well in the dryer grasslands. Often the various plant communities overlap and in some "sweet spots" the environment may be able to support three or more plant communities. The list of plants was created using a species list of dominant plants within Wilder Ranch prepared by the Inventory, Monitoring, and Assessment Program, Natural Resources Division in 2002. To help better identify the species, the list was divided into six plant communities.

The six plant communities are:
- Coastal Strand
- Wetlands
- Redwoods and Evergreen Forests
- Prairie Grasslands
- Chaparral
- Cultivated

Sand verbena (*Abronia umbellata*)

Plant Community: Coastal Strand

Native: Yes

Description: The Sand verbena is a nice perennial native living within the coastal strand ecosystem. It favors beaches and sand dunes and if left undisturbed will create a rather striking carpet like groundcover. It does bloom yearlong, carrying clusters of pink wonderful smelling flowers. This plant is considered uncommon so please be careful when treading in areas where the verbena may be growing.

Beach-bur (*Ambrosia chamissonis*)

Plant Community: Coastal Strand

Native: Yes

Description: Beach bur, also known as Silver Burr Ragweed, does come from the ragweed family and is found on most of the Pacific coastline from Alaska to Baja California. It is a perennial herb found along the coastal strand up to elevations of 82 feet. As its name suggests, Beach-bur drops rather sharp little burrs on the beach making barefoot walking unpleasant when encountered.

Sea rocket (*Cakile maritima*)

Plant Community: Coastal Strand

Native: No

Description: The Sea rocket or European sea rocket is widespread in Europe and is an introduced species in North America from the United Kingdom. This annual is quite common and is a member of the mustard family growing in clumps or mounds in sandy beaches. It gets its Latin name "C. maritima" because the corky brown fruits it produces actually float, thus the plant makes good use of the seas to help disperse itself.

Beach primrose (*Camissonia cheiranthifolia*)

Plant Community: Coastal Strand

Native: Yes

Description: If ever there was a plant that just seems to say, "Hi! Welcome to the North Coast", the Beach primrose is one of them. Soft yellow flowers that seem to cling fragilely to the shifting sands, the plant is actually well adapted to its environment which extends through coastal California and Oregon. It is also known as the Beach Suncup, the plant is a member of the Evening primrose family and is easily spotted by its four petal flower configuration that open in the cool morning coastal air.

Fig-marigold (*Carpobrotus chilensis*)

Plant Community: Coastal Strand, Prairie, Chaparral

Native: No

Description: A succulent far from home, this plant (also known as the Sea Fig and similar to the ice plant) originates from Africa. How it got here is up the speculation but it is generally believed to have been introduced during early Spanish settlement. At this point, it is considered an invasive species and is found in every coastal county in California. It grows fast, spreading as it grows which in turn chokes out native species. A small stem fragment can regenerate itself into an entire new plant, making it difficult to control. This is an actively controlled plant at Wilder Ranch SP.

Saltgrass (*Distichlis spicata*)

Plant Community: Coastal Strand

Native: Yes

Description: Saltgrass is quite common along coast-lines and gets its name because it has the ability to expel excess salts via salt glands. For this reason it has been used for pastures that are irrigated with saline wa-ters, where it thrives and can be used as grazing material for both horses and cattle. For early colonists along the Atlantic coast, saltgrass was their primary source of hay and thus played its own role in the founding of the United States.

Woolly sunflower
(*Eriophyllum staechadifolium*)

Plant Community: Coastal Strand

Native: Yes

Description: This delightful flower is
a small but sprawling plant that is a
member of the daisy family. Its size
does vary with the conditions it grows
in; harsher coastal winds will produce
a smaller plant. It produces clusters of golden yellow flowers.

This plant is a major component in plant restoration projects due to its fast
growth and ability to spread.

Storksbill (*Erodium sp.*)

Plant Community: Coastal strand, Chaparral,
Prairie Grassland

Native: No

Description: Erodium is a pretty flower
that looks at home in California, but alas it
originated from the Mediterranean. It is also
known as Filarees or Heron's Bill. There are
about 60 species in all within the genus.

The Storksbill is quite an invasive plant and is especially damaging in desert
regions due to its overall water consumption and ability to spread. The plant's
seeds look a lot like a stork's bill, hence the name. When the seed drops from
the plant, the spiked "bill" will land on the ground and become dry. When
the bill part is wetted, it will curl like a corkscrew and literally drill itself into
the ground.

California buckwheat
(Eriogonum latifolium)

Plant Community: Coastal Strand

Native: Yes

Description: A common sight amongst
the coastal strand ecosystem, this perennial herb has a cluster of pinkish
flowers extended at the end of each branch. The plant itself is highly variable
in size, which is not uncommon for plants that are required to adapt to the
persistent and often harsh climes of the California coast.

Cattail (*Typha latifolia*)

Plant Community: Wetlands

Native: Yes

Description: The native cattail, as appealing as it is to see poking out of marshy wetlands, is considered a noxious weed in Australia. It is native in every state with the exception of Hawaii, who shares Australia's feelings as an invasive species. It is always found near water and the rhizomes are actually edible if properly prepared. That being said, the plant will absorb pollutants and is not advised to try in urban areas. The roots have been used in some cultures as a poultice for burns and wounds.

Stinging nettle (*Urtica dioica*)

Plant Community: Wetlands

Native: Yes

Description: If you've ever brushed against the stinging nettle, the odd burning feeling is one you will never forget. If you haven't been so "lucky", keep hiking, your day will come. The plant is covered with hundreds of hollow stinging hairs on its leaves and stems, each one acting like hypodermic needles ready to inject a cocktail of histamines and other chemicals that overall make the affected area feel like it's on fire. While the sting's reaction to the skin is harmless, you may see visible bumps on the affected area.

It is possible to touch stinging nettles without being stung. The hairs grow in one direction, upward along the stalk and outward along the leaves. Grasping the plant in the direction of growth will push the needles down rather than prick the user. If the technique didn't work, there are plenty of treatments, including lemon juice, calamine lotion or simply cursing at the author while waiting for the pain to go away has also proven effective. The best treatment (and the only one known to truly work) is to rub the underside of a Swordfern on the affected area.

Beyond being painful, stinging nettle is also used as a food and medicine. It is a folk remedy for arthritis. As a food, perhaps its greatest accolade is given at the Stinging Nettle Eating Championships in Dorset, England suggesting what happens to a society after centuries of eating bland food. The championship started in the 1980's when a farmer argued he would eat any neighboring nettle stalk that was taller than his.

A Stinging Nettle Poem

Tender handed stroke the nettle and it will sting you for your pain, but grasp it as a man of mettle and soft as silk it will remain!

Common bulrush or tule (*Schoenoplectus acutus*)

Plant Community: Redwood and Mixed Evergreen Forest

Native: Yes

Description: Common in freshwater marshes across North America, this plant has a thick rounded green stem growing up to 10 feet in height and producing clustered pale brown flowers. Tules play an important role in the

marsh ecosystem providing a more stable environment for other plants to take hold. Tules once lined the shores of Tulare Lake, once the largest freshwater lake west of the Mississippi until it was drained in the 20th century for agriculture. The expression "out in the tules" derives from early settlers to the newly drained lake bed and was meant to express a place where no one would want to live. As stated earlier, the Ohlone used the tule extensively to build sleeping quarters and fishing boats.

Red alder (*Alnus rubra*)

Plant Community: Redwood and Mixed Evergreen Forest

Native: Yes

Description: The Red Alder is the largest of the alders in North America and can grow to over 100 feet in height. It can be distinguished by the underside of its leaves, which have edges that are turned inward.

In California, the deciduous broadleaf tree is found along the Pacific coast, rarely extending more than 100 miles inland from its shores. It is usually the first to begin growing after a major burn as it produces up to a million seeds per hectacre, making it one of the more prolific seed producers. The red alder is used as a dye, as the preferred wood for smoking salmon, woodworking, and a restoration plant option in burned, heavily logged or heavily mined areas.

Arroyo willow (*Salix lasiolepis*)

Plant Community: Redwood and Mixed Evergreen Forest, Riparian

Native: Yes

Description: This is a common treelike shrub found within most of the coastal ranges with Northern California. It is a deciduous plant growing up to 33 feet tall. The shoots are recognized as yellowish brown and very hairy when young. The Arroyo Willow flowers in the spring with yellow catkins (Dutch for "kitten" as catkins resemble a kitten's tail).

Red elderberry
(*Sambucus racemosa*)

Plant Community: Redwood and Mixed Evergreen Forest

Native: Yes

Description: This treelike shrub can grow up to 18 feet tall and is found along creeks and other moist wooded areas. Many parts of this plant are poisonous and were used traditionally to induce vomiting.

Tanoak (*Lithocarpus densiflorus*)

Plant Community: Redwood and Mixed Evergreen Forest

Native: Yes

Description: The tanoak is easily spotted with its serrated elongated leaves. The tree gets its name from its tannin rich bark, which was used for tanning leather in the 18th century. While modern tanning mech-

anisms replaced its use in the leather industry, it is still considered for its timber, with roughly 50 million board feet of sustainable forestlands in northern California.

Madrone (*Arbutus menziesii*)

Plant Community: Redwood and Mixed Evergreen Forest

Native: Yes

Description: The Madrone has a rather unique alternative name, the refrigerator tree. Since the tree does not have an external layer of bark, what is touchable is living energy producing tree, a great majority of which involves the transport of water and other nutrients up from its roots to its stems. This gives the tree a cooling effect. As noted, the Madrone is easily spotted by its paper thin bark that is constantly shedding itself in brown sheets. The Madrone is in decline as it depends greatly on forest fires for the germination of its seeds. With wildfires being increasingly under the control of man, the Madrone has reduced opportunity to sprout new trees. Within Wilder, the berries of the Madrone are eaten by many birds and mammals including the mule deer that will even eat the young shoots.

California buckeye (*Aesculus californica*)

Plant Community: Redwood and Mixed Evergreen Forest

Native: Yes

Description: The California Buckeye (also seen as the California Horse-chestnut) is the only native buckeye in California. The buckeye is easily identified by its broad dark green leaves that can appear to have a downy surface, especially in the spring. The flowers, large panicles that stand upright, are white to pale pink and offer a sweet scent. In the spring especially the Buckeye's almost fluorescent green leaves will stand out against the lesser green trees. In summer, these same leaves will turn a rusty brown, again contrasting with the now greener oaks.

The California Buckeye is found along most of the coast in California up to Oregon and as far east as the foothills of the Sierras. It can grow in a wide range of areas, from moist semi-shaded canyon bottoms to dry south facing slopes. Its bark is often home to lichens and mosses.

The nuts of the buckeye are actually poisonous and certain Native American tribes would use the toxins to catch fish. They would grind up a number of the seeds and pour them into streams where fish were present. The fish would float to the surface or otherwise become stunned enough for easy picking. They were also known to eat the leached nuts as part of their diet.

Douglas fir (*Pseudotsuga menziesii*)

Plant Community: Redwood and Mixed Evergreen Forest

Native: Yes

Description: The Douglas fir has a wide range and is contiguous from the western Cascades to the Pacific Coast Ranges down as far south as Santa Barbara County. The tree's Latin name menziesii comes from Archibald Menzies, a Scottish naturalist who first documented the tree on Vancouver Island in 1791. This is quite an honor for Menzies as the Douglas fir is now considered the most commercially important tree in the North American west.

The Douglas fir's rapid growth and high yield make it a darling of the timber industry. It dries without warping and is a solid "go to" wood for dimensional lumber, timbers, pilings and plywood. It can be treated with Creosote and used in outside decking, marine structures and landscaping. It is also the most popular choice for the family Christmas tree in North America.

Coast redwood (*Sequoia sempervirens*)

Plant Community: Redwood and Mixed Evergreen Forest

Native: Yes

Description: The Coastal redwood is the tallest living tree on the planet. From the same family, the Giant Sequoia redwood (Sequoiadendron giganteum), is the largest. The tallest redwood Hyperion resides in Redwood National Park and is just over 379 feet in height.

The Coast Redwood occupies a narrow strip of land along the Pacific coast of North America, with a range starting in San Luis Obispo, California extending as far north as the southernmost tip of Oregon. They greatly depend on moisture from coastal fog and their small leaves have evolved to become quite adept at capturing the coastal mist for their water supply. It is not uncommon to stand in a grove of redwoods on a foggy morning and feel the cool drops of "redwood rain" as the trees capture and release the fog layer to feed their roots.

The Latin word for the tree, "sempervirens", means "everlasting" and this is not far from the truth. The trees can live to be over 2200 years old with many of the old growth stands exceeding 600 years. The trees are well adapted to survival; they are able to better withstand fires, are rich in insect repelling tannins and have an ability to literally pull water out of the air.

Perhaps the agedness of the coastal redwood is what gives it perhaps its most remarkable characteristic, majesty. Standing in a grove of the tallest living organism that has been alive for hundreds or even thousands of years brings a sense of awe and wonder to anyone who stops to ponder.

Knobcone pine (*Pinus attenuata*)

Plant Community: Redwood and Mixed Evergreen Forest

Native: Yes

Description: The Knobcone pine is common from southern Oregon to Baja California and is most abundant in northern California. It prefers mild climates and dry rocky mountain soils and can be a shrub if the soil is especially poor. The leaves are needlelike as is typical for a pine and the mature bark is a dark gray red brown with flat scaly ridges.

California Bay (*Umbellularia californica*) (aka – Pepperwood, Bay Laurel, Bay Tree, Oregon Myrtle)

Plant Community: Redwood and Mixed Evergreen Forest

Native: Yes

Description: The California Bay is a hardwood tree native to the California region. The tree's aromatic leaves are similar and actually stronger than bay leaves and it may be mistaken for the Bay Laurel. The leaves of the California bay are smooth edged and lance shaped as are the Bay Laurel. However, the California bay will typically have narrower leaves and lack the crinkled margins and vein like quality of the Bay Laurel.

The California Bay was used by many Native American tribes to cure many ailments including headaches, sore throat and clearing of the sinuses. Ironically, the purified oil of the Bay Laurel is well documented for inducing headaches rather than curing it, thus proving that old world remedies and science don't always see eye to eye. Both the flesh and inner kernel of the fruit was used in the Native American diet. The fruit is similar to the avocado and the large pit was roasted and eaten whole. The flavor notes of this nut include dark chocolate, coffee and burnt popcorn. The leaves are used even today in pet bedding to repel fleas.

Santa Cruz mountain oak
(*Quercus parvula var. shrevei*)

Plant Community: Redwood and Mixed Evergreen Forest

Native: Yes

Description: This evergreen oak is native and highly variable, sometimes appearing as a shrub. The dark green leaves are similar but smaller to the California Buckeye.

Poison oak
(*Toxicodendron diversilobum*)

Plant Community: Redwood and Mixed Evergreen Forest

Native: Yes

Description: There is an old adage for Poison Oak, "Leaves of three, leave them be." While there are several species that share the same ecosystem and characteristics of Poison Oak, this is a good rule of thumb as the plants toxic effects are not only irritating, they can be long lasting (up to 2-3 weeks).

Poison Oak effects are actually an allergic reaction to the plants surface oil, urushiol and develop over time. There are cases where people have been repeatedly exposed to the plant and did not develop any adverse side effects. Yet with each exposure the chances of getting a rash from poison oak increase. When in an area with poison oak, it is important to minimize both exposure to the plant and any animals that are on the walk with you. Fido is immune to urushiol but the oil can easily rub off on him, passing it to you. Wash up thoroughly with soap and cold water if you feel you or your pet have been in contact.

Effects include severe itching along the affected area, inflammation, colorless bumps and blistering if overly scratched. In the late fall and winter, the plant loses its leaves, however the branches are still loaded with urushiol. There have been cases of campers using poison oak branches to toast marshmallows or hot dogs which resulted in hospitalization. Burning poison oak creates the highest threat as the smoke can bathe the victim's skin as well as their lungs and throat.

The plant itself is highly variable and can be a dense shrub, a tree, a vine and even a sprawling low shrub. The leaves are divided into three and are scalloped and do resemble that of true oaks.

Himalayan blackberry (*Rubus discolor*)

Plant Community: Redwood and Mixed Evergreen Forest

Native: No

Description: The Himalayan blackberry is a non-native plant coming from Asia. The species was introduced to North America for its fruit production in 1885. The fruit is similar to the common blackberries but is larger and sweeter. Today it is considered both an invasive species and a delight amongst hikers who recognize it as one of the few fruits they can eat on the trail without concern. The plant itself is hard to contain and has become a widespread species throughout the Pacific Northwest.

Blackberry (*Rubus ursinus*)

Plant Community: Redwood and Mixed Evergreen Forest

Native: Yes

Description: The Blackberry is similar to the Himalayan Black-berry and can be distinguished by having a smaller fruit but most notably the flower's petals are nar-row compared to the Himalayan blackberry. This was a staple fruit for Native Americans. Alternate names for this species include California blackberry, Douglas blackberry and Pacific dewberry.

Wood Fern (*Dryopteris arguta*)

Plant Community: Redwood and Mixed Evergreen Forest

Native: Yes

Description: The wood fern is a common sight in redwood forests as well as other evergreen forests. It is widely distributed and is found throughout California, Oregon, Washington and even western Canada.

Swordfern (*Polystichum munitum*)

Plant Community: Redwood and Mixed Evergreen Forest

Native: Yes

Description: The Sword fern is a native of North America and is most abundant along the Pacific Coast. Common to ferns but very notable to the Swordfern are the two rows of brown sori on the underside of the leaf frond. These spores are an ancient but still effective means of reproduction.

One interesting side note is its use for stinging nettle attacks. Simply rub the underside spores of a Swordfern into the affected area to get instant relief. As the two plants typically grow together, a cure for the fiery sting should be nearby.

Silver hairgrass (*Aira caryophyllea*)

Plant Community: Prairie Grasslands

Native: No

Description: This non native grass is identified by its silvery sheen on its spikelets before it dries and becomes a straw color. It is one of the species of bunchgrass, coming originally from Europe.

Quaking grass (*Briza maxima*)

Plant Community: Prairie

Native: No

Description: The seeds of this non-native grass are so unique that it has inspired a number of common names, including Blowfly Grass, Rattlesnake Grass, Shelly Grass as well as Big Quaking, Great Quaking, Large Quaking just plain Quaking Grass. The seeds are not only edible but available to purchase from nurseries where folks grow the plant as an ornamental. When fully dried on the stem, the Quaking Grass is easily recognized by the gentle hollow rustling sound it makes as the wind touches the seed pods.

Bromes (*Bromus sp.*)

Plant Community: Prairie

Native: Some native

Description: The only place you won't find this non-native grass in California is in the heat of the desert. It has a number of names, including cheatgrass, downy brome, and military grass. Preferring temperate climates, it is found on every continent except Antartica. It is so widespread the Bromus most likely has plans to take over the world one day. It is typically a short grass with bright green seed that reddens as it matures. The seeds are quite good at catching in clothing and shoes. For that reason, the grass may go by other names that cannot be listed here.

Ben Lomond spineflower (Chorizanthe pungens var. hartwegiana)

Plant Community: Coastal Strand, Prairie

Native: Yes

Description: The Ben Lomond spineflower is found only in the Santa Cruz Mountains north of Santa Cruz. It is listed as an endangered species so please tread carefully if you see any. They are typically found along the coastline and in the coastal hills above. Depending on conditions it will grow in an erect fashion or sometimes prostrate, spreading up to 1.5 feet.

Wild oatgrass (*Danthonia californica*)

Plant Community: Prairie Grasslands

Native: Yes

Description: Wild oatgrass also goes by the name California oatgrass though it is a common grass found from Chile to Canada. The leaves are flat and are sometimes hairy and the plant itself will grow in bunches with stems reaching up to 3 feet in height. It prefers moist areas and is usually found in meadows and airy forests. Researchers have discovered that Wild oatgrass can actually live to be hundreds of years old.

Fennel (*Foeniculum vulgare*)

Plant Community: Prairie Grassland

Native: No

Description: This plant originated on the shores of the Mediterranean but has found itself growing all over the world, including California. The plant is highly invasive and Wilder SP has been controlling it for some time. It prefers dry soils near the coast. Its main characteristic is its aroma, which is similar to anise or licorice. It is one of the three main herbs used in the preparation of absinthe, a popular alcoholic tonic in France in the 19th century and a hipster elixir in this century. Dried fennel seed is commonly used in cooking, especially in the preparation of Italian sausages and some risottos. In India it is reputed to improve eyesight and is found as an alternative to the after dinner mint in some Indian restaurants.

Purple needlegrass
(*Nassella pulchra*)

Plant Community: Prairie Grassland and Chaparral

Native: Yes

Description: Purple needlegrass is a common native to California, ranging along its coast, valleys and deeper into the Sierra Foothills. The plant produces a remarkable 227 pounds of seeds per acre. It supported Native American groups and is so widespread it was named the State Grass of California in 2004. One great quality of this native is it actually suppresses invasive plants, which only means that it does a better job at surviving than the plant species that came from other parts of the globe.

Small fescue (*Vulpia bromoides/myuros*)

Plant Community: Prairie Grassland

Native: No

Description: This non-native grass originally came to California from the Hawaiian Islands however it was originally native to Europe and North Africa. It is found primarily in the western United States and northern Mexico.

Poison hemlock (*Conium maculatum*)

Plant Community: Redwood and Mixed Evergreen Forest

Native: No

Description: If the common name wasn't a "dead giveaway", yes this is the same poison hemlock Socrates drank after being charged with corrupting people with his philosophy. Hemlock prefers poorly drained moist soils and is found along roadsides and edges of cultivated fields. While there are medicinal uses of the plant, since improper use results in death, its best to leave the plant alone. All parts of the plant are poisonous to both humans and animals. It is not poisonous to the touch, but is if it is consumed. The main toxin in hemlock is coniine which disrupts the central nervous system resulting in respiratory collapse and death. If hemlock is accidently ingested, getting the victim to a hospital where artificial respiration can be applied can save their life.

Box elder (*Acer negundo var. californicum*)

Plant Community: Redwood and Mixed Evergreen Forest

Native: Yes

Description: Also known as the California Boxelder, this member of the Maple family is fast growing and fairly short lived, having several trunks that combine to make off trail hiking a challenge. The subspecies californicum has larger leaves than the main species and are velvety to the touch. The "helicopter seeds" can often be seen whirling from the trees in the fall.

Coast Live Oak (*Quercus agrifolia*)

Plant Community: Chaparral

Native: Yes

Description: Coast Live Oak is a highly variable evergreen oak. It can be shrub like or tree like and seems to adapt to its surroundings as it needs to. It can be found as far east as the Sierra Nevada and as far south as northern Baja California.

Its Latin name literally means "sharp-leaved oak" and indeed the leaves are rather sharp. The Ohlone and many other Native Americans relied on the Coastal Live Oak acorns as a dietary staple. The great cities of San Diego and San Francisco began as great oak woodlands of this noble tree. The tree has inspired artists, shipbuilders, pioneers and modern hikers who are lucky enough to have the glow of one in the midst of their travels in the late afternoon sun.

Coyote Brush (*Baccharis pilularis*)

Plant Community: Chaparral

Native: Yes

Description: This shrub is also called Chaparral Broom and Bush Baccharis. Another native, it is a hardy plant that is considered a secondary pioneer plant in the chaparral communities. As a result, it is an indicator of a more established ecosystem that has not undergone a fire or significant grazing. The establishment of the Coyote Brush helps pave the way for other native species such as the California bay and coastal live oak, which will eventually dominate and replace the shrub as the ecosystem matures in the absence of fire or grazing. It will eventually outcompete native grasses and shrubs and is periodically controlled by the parks with fire.

(Sticky Monkey) Bush monkeyflower (*Mimulus aurantiacus*)

Plant Community: Chaparral, mixed evergreen, scrub

Native: Yes

Description: Also known as the Orange bush monkeyflower, this shrub is easily recognized by its deep green and sticky leaves and tubular flowers. It thrives in many soils, wet, dry, sandy or rocky. The Monkeyflower is the host plant for the Checkerspot butterfly, which is federally threatened but not uncommon to see them on this sticky shrub.

(Blue Blossom Ceanothus) California lilac (*Ceanothus cuneatus*)

Plant Community: Chaparral

Native: Yes

Description: The California lilac is a native spreading bush that grows low to the ground. With white flowers that produce small round capsules with horns that explode, propelling the three shiny dark seeds some distance. Harvester ants will cache the seeds which require fire for germination.

The lilac described here is the least common of the ceanothus species found in Wilder SP, making up only 1-2% of the species distribution. Ceanothus thyrsiflorus or blue blossom ceanothus makes up over 80% and Ceanothus papilosus makes up about 10% of the distribution.

Bonny Doon Manzanita
(*Arctostaphylos silvicola*)

Plant Community: Chaparral

Native: Yes

Description: The word manzanita was first coined by the Spanish who saw the fruits and remarked they looked like "little apples", which in Spanish is (as you may have guessed) manzanita. A true local, the Bonny Doon Manzanita is endemic to Santa Cruz County.

It is listed as a shrub but can grow to 20 feet in height and has many characteristics similar to a tree. The bark is dark red and smooth to the touch. It can particularly artful after a rain.

Woollyleaf manzanita
(*Arctostaphylos tomentosa var. crustacea and var. crinite*)

Plant Community: Chaparral

Native: Yes

Description: The woolly-leaf Manzanita is low lying spreading shrub that is typically wider than it is tall. The flowers are pinkish white while the fruits are a reddish stonefruit.

California sagebrush (*Artemisia californica*)

Plant Community: Coastal Strand, Chaparral

Native: Yes

Description: The California Sage, with its pleasant aroma, is one of the fonder members of the plant community. It grows primarily in the dry chaparral foothills of the California Coast Ranges and is a native of the state. Amongst its unique qualities, the plant relies on wildfires for seed germination and produces a natural inhibiting chemical that keeps other plants from growing too close to the shrub.

Oats (*Avena sp.*)

Plant Community: Prairie Grasslands, Chaparral

Native: No

Description: Before you read this and think you can harvest the oats in Wilder Ranch State Park, it's worth noting that these are Wild Oats and are hard to harvest. The oats in your oatmeal are known as the Common oat and produce a far greater yield than the ones Wilder can provide. Wild oats are actually invasive to cereal crops and since both varieties are grasses and similar, eradication is difficult. That being said, if you do find yourself stuck in Wilder for an extended period of time due to a zombie apocalypse or other similar scenario, the wild oat versions are edible.

The problematic nature of Wild Oats in the production of grains is long standing and the term "Sowing wild oats" was first noted in 1542 by Thomas Beccon, a Protestant clergyman in Norfolk, England. Beccon used it in reference to an unprofitable activity since trying to weed out wild oats in a field of common oats is a meticulous task. Oat grains then gained the reputation as an "invigorating" food. Over time the meaning of "sowing wild oats" changed to indicate a sexual liaison ending in an out of wedlock child.

Italian thistle (*Carduus pycnocephalus*)

Plant Community: Chaparral

Native: No

Description: Originally
from the Mediterra-
nean, the Italian thistle
is considered a moderate
invasive species by the
California Invasive Plant
Council. It loves to grow
under oak trees and cre-
ates an unnatural fire haz-
ard for the trees. It can
get quite dense in growth
crowding out native vege-
tation. Mowing this plant
down isn't effective as it
will grow back unless the
root is removed at least 4
inches below the ground.

Bull thistle (*Cirsium vulgare*)

Plant Community: Chaparral

Native: No

Description: The bull thistle (aka spear
thistle) has as part of its scientific name
the word "vulgare", which despite an
easy connection to the word vulgar; it
actually is Latin for "common". Whether the Bull thistle is vulgar or common
or both, it is considered an injurious
and invasive weed. It is one of those
plants that have built up a wonderful ar-
senal of defense, spiny leaves that poke
out of a long spear shaped stem, even
its redeemable purple flower sits atop of
a globe of spines. The Bull thistle will
be the first to colonize bare disturbed
ground and is unpalatable to most animals. It is related to the artichoke.

Blue gum eucalyptus (*Eucalyptus globulus*)

Plant Community: Chaparral

Native: no

Description: Just about everyone knows that the Eucalyptus came over from Australia. It's a little odd that this is part of California culture but the many other non native plants aren't. This is most likely due to the size of the tree, which can grow as high as 180 feet tall. But there is a back story on this plant. It was brought over from Australia in the 1850's partly because of its rapid growth rate and subsequent use as timber for the railroad industry. Unfortunately the railroad men who recognized its ability to grow rapidly didn't have the foresight that it would do just that and is now considered an invasive species. They also didn't realize the wood makes horrible railroad ties. It has a tendency to twist and split as it dries.

While the Eucalyptus does not come from California, it does offer a nice source of nectar and pollen for the California bees and its unique aroma does invoke thoughts of comfort and relaxation for most. Many parks, such as Angel Island SP and Wilder Ranch SP have developed programs to eradicate the tree from the park's territory altogether.

Chaparral pea (*Pickeringia Montana*)

Plant Community: Chaparral

Native: Yes

Description: This is one of the few natives of the legume family and was named after naturalist Charles Pickering. Like most legumes (pea family), the bright magenta flowers bear pea pods. It is found only in California.

It does have some nasty thorns so be careful. Folks have asked if it is edible, given it is a pea. Deer love to nibble their way around the thorns, it is not known if it is edible to the human species.

Coffeeberry (*Rhamnus californica*) (syn. *Frangula californica*)

Plant Community: Chaparral

Native: Yes

Description: This is a common plant that is often referred to as the California buckthorn or coffeeberry as the berries contain seeds that resemble coffee beans. The plant prefers windy or exposed areas but has been seen in sheltered canyons individually. The plant is found in coastal chaparral areas and grows to about 6-7 feet. The fruit of this evergreen shrub was gathered by the Ohlone for both its sweet flavor and as laxative.

Cultivated

Brussels sprouts (*Brassica oleracea var. gemmifera*)

Plant Community: Cultivated

Native: No

Description: When you think of Oak Chaparral, Redwood or Coastal Strand ecosystems, Brussels sprouts don't typically come to mind. However, it is difficult to represent Wilder Ranch in its fullest sense without pausing for a moment to discuss this vegetable.

The Brussels sprout is so abundantly grown on the Wilder Ranch State Park it makes up 12% of the nation's production. The agricultural preserve is leased by the state to various farmers. One of the longest partnerships with this land goes to the Rodoni family, who has been farming Brussels sprouts since Dante Rodoni and his wife Andreina moved onto the Wilder land in 1935.

While saying that 12% of Brussels sprouts comes from Wilder is impressive, the fact that so much of the vegetable is grown in such a small lot speaks to its popularity as a vegetable. Still, they have been noted as containing a chemical called indole-3-carbinol, which has been found to boost DNA repair in cells and actually block cancer. If you want to take advantage of their health properties, it's best to steam or microwave them rather than boil the vegetable.

Fauna

Orange Blossom - One of the Treasured Non Native Fauna at Wilder Ranch

The amount of wildlife in Wilder is stunning in both number and variety. There are numerous rodents, insectivores, coastal marine mammals, rabbits, deer, foxes, coyotes, bobcats and mountain lions all coexisting in the park.

In 2002 an extensive species list was performed by Research Analyst Pat Gilbert on behalf of the California Department of Parks and Recreation Natural Resources Division. Prior to this study, very little was known about the mammalian diversity and quantity within the park. Their methods produced a very thorough species list which was used to catalog the fauna shown here.

Salamanders (*Caudata*)

Rough-skinned newts (*Taricha granulosa*)

Conservation Status: Least Concern

Description: The Rough skinned newt is fairly common especially around shores of still ponds and moist areas. They are fairly slow moving and can be quite docile. While this makes them easy to catch don't let their benign appearance fool you. These guys exude a toxin called tarichatoxin that can cause paralysis and even death. Respect the newt.

Tarichatoxin is the same toxin found in pufferfish, some toads, certain angelfish and several sea stars. The first recorded poisoning due to tarichatoxin was from the crew of Captain James Cook in 1774. Apparently the crew dined on some pufferfish and then fed the scraps to their pigs. The crew experienced numbness and shortness of breath while all the pigs, who ate the more toxic body parts, were found dead the following morning. Tarichatoxin is the main ingredient used in Voodoo magic to turn humans into "zombies".

Symptoms start with a slight numbness of the lips and tongue followed by paralysis of facial muscles. Second stage symptoms are noticed as increasing paralysis. As there is no known antivenom, treatment involves stomach pumping, activated charcoal ingestion and life support.

There was a case of one man who on a dare ate a newt and died shortly thereafter. The toxin must be ingested so if you do accidently touch one and then read this, wash your hands immediately and it goes without saying, don't put your hands in your mouth. If contact has been made and in doubt, seek medical attention.

Now that you have a bit more respect for the newt, here's a brief synopsis for this rather cute little water creature. They are carnivorous, eating insects, spiders and amphibians. They have a strong sense of smell and are able to find concentrations of hatchling tadpoles. They have also been observed stalking their prey.

They will migrate to breeding waters such as still ponds beginning in October creating at times amazing amounts of newts in a single body of water (up to 5000 per hectare have been reported). Females will lay eggs which will develop into a pole, metamorphosing by the next summer into juveniles who then become terrestrial and migrate some distance away. They reach sexual maturity after 2-4 years.

Slugs (*Gastropoda*)

Banana slug (*Ariolamax californicus, Ariolimax columbianus and Ariolimax dolichophallus*)

Conservation Status: Least Concern

Description: The Slender Banana Slug is indeed the official mascot of the UC Santa Cruz "Slugs" and so a State Park that harbors them this close to the campus deserves a nod to this slimy little fellow. They are typically bright yellow and like all members of the mollusk family do not do well if dehydrated. The Banana slug deals with this by producing a slime that can absorb water in incredible quantities, up to 100 times its initial volume. Trying to wash the slime off of one's hands will demonstrate this as it is very difficult to remove. It's best to wipe the slime off with a dry towel or rub your hands together until the slime rolls up into a rubber cement like ball.

Species include the California, Pacific and Slender banana slug. Some slugs do develop black spots to the point of looking almost entirely black. It is the second largest terrestrial slug in the world growing to over 9 inches in length. A close look will reveal two sets of tentacles. The larger ones on top detect light and movement while the lower ones detect chemicals. They live to eat leaves, animal droppings and other dead plant material and turn the food into rich organic matter.

Opossums (*Didelphimorphia*)

Virginia Opossum (*Didelphis virginiana*)

Conservation Status: Least Concern

Description:

"My love is an opossum, unexpected,

oddly shaped, close to the ground

and somehow resolute, certain of itself,

and you." – quote from Richard Beben's What the Heart Weighs

Opossums make up the largest order of marsupials in the Western Hemisphere and the Virginia Opossum, found here in Cowell was the first animal to be named an Opossum, back in 1610. If you caught that opossums are marsupials and thought kangaroo, you'd be correct; they do come from the same Infraclass and share in the same "baby in a pouch" characteristics.

Opossums are about the size of a large house cat, nocturnal, solitary and great opportunists. It is not terribly shy within the range of humans, using the cover of night to top over garbage cans and eat pet food. Opossums actually have opposable "thumbs" on their back feet as well as 50 teeth, the most of any mammal in North America.

Opossums are omnivorous, which adds to their opportunistic qualities, which is to say, they aren't picky in what they eat, including known cases of eating each other. They live about two years, which is typical for marsupials. The opossums reproduce similar to other mammals however the young are born at a very early stage. The young is then faced with its first challenge, to find its way into the pouch (marsupium) for food and all the comforts of mom. They make the pouch their home between 70-125 days before getting the boot. Once they do leave the pouch, one can image the young getting a suitcase and some general advice on how to make it on their own in the world however this particular point is well debated and is considered by some as being completely fictional whimsy on behalf of the author.

The notion that opossums will play dead is not a myth. If threatened, they will "play possum", mimicking the appearance and even smell of a dead or dying animal. What is interesting is that the opossum actually faints, presumably out of fear and does not consciously pretend to be dead. When their brain triggers the physiological response, the lips will draw back barring the teeth, saliva will form around the mouth, the eyes will close and a foul smell will exude from their nether regions. One can actually pick them up by their stiff, curled tail. They will remain unconscious for 40 minutes to up to 4 hours.

Insectivores (*Insectivora*)

Trowbridge's Shrew (*Sorex trowbridgii*)

Conservation Status: Least Concern

Description: Shrew's in general are not mice, nor are they rodents, though the Trowbridge Shrew does look like a mouse with a long nose. What makes them different is shrews have sharp spike like teeth whereas the mouse has more blunt gnawing teeth. These sharper teeth are used primarily for catching insects, which puts the shrew in the category of insectivore (insect eater).

Shrews have horrible eyesight but make up for it with a great sense of smell and hearing. They prefer insects and worms but will augment their diets with seeds and nuts as well. They are very active, always looking for food to satisfy their extremely high metabolisms.

While the shrew does not hibernate, it does enter into a state of torpor which can result in a winter weight loss of up to 50% of their body weight.

While the Trowbridge Shrew itself is not known to do this, some shrews can echolocate (use sound to navigate by). The Trowbridge Shrew is venomous, which is very unusual for a mammal. It carries its venom through grooves in its teeth which are lethal enough to kill 200 mice. It is rare for humans to encounter the bite of the shrew.

Perhaps the biggest claim to fame of the shrew is that it's brain is 10% of its body mass, the greatest of any mammal, including us, who have a mere 2.5% brain to body mass ratio. Fortunately, it appears that this ratio is not an indication of actual intelligence. If it were, we would most certainly be ruled by echo-locating shrews with vampire like qualities.

Shrew-mole (*Neurotrichus gibbsii*)

Conservation Status: Least Concern

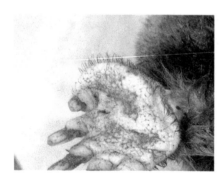

Description: This little guy is the smallest North American mole. It has the long nosed characteristics of the shrew, which gives it half its name. Moles however are subterranean purists, preferring life in the underground. They are highly adapted to living in holes to the point that they have a higher tolerance for carbon dioxide than other mammals. They also have an extra thumb (which would give them the ability to give four thumbs up if they were able to rate movies). The extra thumb and lack of sharp needle like teeth are what separate them from the true shrew.

Moles love earthworms and other insect like creatures they can find in the dirt. They, like shrews will augment their diet with nuts. Also like shrews, they have a venom in their saliva which allows them to paralyze and stockpile earthworms, creating underground larders. Researchers have found such larders with over a thousand earthworms in them. The mole will actually pull an earthworm through their paws to squeeze out the collected earth in the worms belly prior to eating it.

Broad-footed Mole (*Scapanus latimanus*)

Conservation Status: Least Concern

Description: The Broad Footed Mole is similar to other moles and are distinguished by having forefeet that are almost as wide as they are long. Other than that, they are very much like the Shrew-Mole.

Bats (*Chiroptera*)

Townsend's Big-eared Bat (*Corynorhinus townsendii*)

Photo: Dave Bunnell

Conservation Status: Least Concern

Description: For most people, bats are cool and scary all at the same time. There is tremendous wonder if you ever see one flying around with near insect like flight precision and tremendous creepiness if you've ever been in a small cave with a bunch of them zipping around your head.

The Townsend's Big Eared Bat gets its name due to its extremely long, flexible ears. Townsend's bat has a uniform body color that is a wood brown, with dark brown wings. They hibernate in the winter, where they huddle in tight clusters to keep themselves warm. Unlike the deep hibernation of bears, the Townsend's bat will wake up frequently to find a warmer part of the pack.

The Townsend's Big-eared bat can live up to 16 years and they mate in the fall where the courtship falls with the male. Like humans, the pups are born pink, naked and helpless. For food, they hunt at night using echolocation to find their prey. Their diet is made up of small insects, including moths and flies.

Hares and Rabbits (*Lagomorpha*)

Brush rabbit (*Sylvilagus bachmani*)

Conservation Status: Least Concern

Description: The Brush rabbit or Western Brush rabbit is one of the cottontail rabbits found in the coastal regions of the west. They hop around from the Columbia River in Oregon to Cabo San Lucas down in Baja, California and as far east as the Sierras.

The brush rabbit is aptly named as it prefers the cover of brush, even in urban areas, as its habitation area. It feeds mainly on grasses, especially clover, which it finds in patches within the brush or in the fringe around it.

Ecologically, the Brush rabbit is a big part of the food chain, being prey for cougars, coyotes, foxes and even raptors and snakes. They use brush cover and when in a pinch will stand in a statue like pose in hopes to blend into their surroundings.

The old adage about rabbits is true for the Brush rabbit. It does mate year round and goes through the gestation process in a short 22 days. A Brush rabbit can have up to five litters a year with one to seven young born per litter.

Audubon's Cottontail (*Sylvilagus audubonii*)

Conservation Status: Least
Concern

Description: The Audubon's
or Desert Cottontail is similar
and as common as the Brush
Rabbit. To tell them apart,
easiest is by the ears; Audubon's Cottontail has the bigger ones. (The Black-tailed
Jackrabbit also has big ears,
but lacks the cottontail). Other than that there are a lot of
similarities between the two
rabbits. They both eat grasses, reproduce like bunnies
and are a rich source of food
amongst the predator types.
The Desert Cottontail does
have a range that extends
much farther east. While the
Brush rabbit ranges as far
east as the Sierra foothills, the
Desert Cottontail lives as far
as central Nevada.

The two rabbits share a lot
more than diet and turf.
Both were first scientifically recognized by two naturalists of the 1800's. Rev-
erend John Bachman and John James Audubon spent a number of months
travelling together and sharing in their knowledge and passion for recording
nature. Together they wrote and illustrated a monumental publication on
mammals called Viviparous Quadrupeds of North America. This book gave
Americans of the mid-19th century their first real look at mammals within
North America including many that are in Henry Cowell. The book became a
go to standard for scholars and armchair naturalists and is today a benchmark
in what was alive then and is extinct now.

By now you are probably saying, this is great and all, but how does this apply
to Brush and Desert Rabbits? Well, given the similarities of these two cottontails, each naturalist, Bachman and Audubon, gave themselves some due
credit when naming them. The Brush Rabbit's Latin name is Sylvilagus bach-
mani while the Desert Rabbit is Sylvilagus audubonii. I imagine they figured
by tying their name to a mammal that reproduces so well, their legacy would
be sure to live on.

Black-tailed Jackrabbit (*Lepus californicus*)

Conservation Status: Least Concern

Description: The Black-tailed Jackrabbit is not a rabbit, nope, it is a hare. So what's a hare then? Well, it's a fast moving rabbit. (At this point, true zoologist readers are cringing, but hey, it's kinda true you guys). Hares have longer legs and are adapted to run up to an amazing 45 mph. If it hops, rabbit. If it runs at "I'm outta here" speeds, hare.

The Black-tailed Jackrabbit is the third largest of the North American hares and occupies mixed shrub-grassland terrains. They have a much larger range then the cottontails, found as far east as Missouri and deeper south into south central Mexico. They do not extend into Canada.

The male Black-tailed Jackrabbit, with its creamy white underside and dark buff fur, reaches sexual maturity at 7 months. Females usually start breeding in their second year. Gestation is between 41 to 47 days giving litter sizes of 2-7 leverets (baby hares).

It is described in the Desert Rabbit section that naturalists Bachman and Audubon had a big hand in the naming of both the Brush and Desert Rabbit. They also coined the term jack rabbit. As the hare has ears resembling the donkey, and as wild donkeys went by the term "jack" (short for jackass), they arrived at the name jackrabbit.

Figure 1: Uncommon Wilder Scene: The Rare "*Lepus jackalopus*"

Rodents (*Rodentia*)

Merriam's Chipmunk (*Tamias merriami*)

Conservation Status: Least Concern

Description: Merriam's chipmunk is one of the cuter members of the rodent family. They live below 8900 feet throughout most of central and southern California as well as northern Baja California. They build nests in logs, stumps, snags and burrows within heavy brush for cover. They are entirely herbivorous, eating acorns, seeds and other nuts. They do cache food for later use and do hibernate.

California Ground Squirrel (*Spermophilus beecheyi*)

Conservation Status: Least Concern

Description: The California Ground Squirrel is found everywhere in the western United States and into Baja California to the south and Washington to the north. The California Ground Squirrel lives in burrows that it excavates. While they will locate their burrows very close to human areas, they do not venture far from the safe haven in the ground they've created. Most of their life is spent within 80 feet of their burrow. While California Ground Squirrels in colder regions will hibernate, the ones at Cowell are active year round.

The biggest predators of the squirrel are rattlesnakes but they are also the favorites of hawks, eagles, raccoons and foxes. The California Ground Squirrel has been known to eat the skins shed by rattlesnakes to disguise their scent and will swish their tail rapidly to give the impression of a larger heat signature to the rattlesnake, who "sees" with its infra red viewing pit organs.

Western gray squirrel (*Sciurus griseus*)

Conservation Status: Least Concern

Description: The Western gray squirrel is a shy tree dweller and will give a high pitched hoarse barking call if it feels threatened. Unlike the California Ground Squirrel, they are not as well adapted to areas that humans frequent and in California are found generally only in mountainous and surrounding foothill communities. The California Ground Squirrel and the Western Gray Squirrel both compete for the same resources.

Botta's Pocket Gopher (*Thomomys bottae*)

Conservation Status: Least Concern

Description: These stocky rodents have large check pouches, which is where the term "pocket" is derived from. Botta's Pocket Gopher is considered a "true" gopher as it largely uses burrowing both for creating a home and for feeding.

The Botta's Gopher is highly adaptable, able to burrow in a wide array of soils, from clays to sands and from dry deserts to high altitude meadows. They spend about 90% of their life underground, eating roots of plants it finds in the over 450 feet of tunnels it will create.

The Pocket Gopher in general is both a pest in urban areas and a benefit in their ability to aerate the soil. For farmers of alfalfa and other grasses, they are of special concern as they have been shown to reduce the productivity of the crops by up to 50%. They are amongst the diets of coyotes, snakes, bobcats, hawks and owls.

Both the common and Latin name of the Botta Pocket Gopher is a nod to world explorer, Archeologist and Naturalist Paul-Emile Botta. The Frenchman Botta was selected as the naturalist for a French financed voyage around the world. He left from the northern city of Le Harve, France and sailed around the Cape Horn in 1826 stopping for some time in the then called "Alta California" where he did some early work in cataloguing mammals of the area. After three years and stops in Hawaii and China, Botta and the crew of the Le Heros returned safe and sound to the same port from which their travels began.

Bad Gopher Jokes

Knock Knock

Who's there!

Gopher!

Gopher who!

Gopher a long walk off a short pier! Knock Knock

Who's there!

Gopher!

Gopher who!

Gopher your gun, Sheriff! Knock Knock

Who's there!

Gopher!

Gopher who!

Gopher broke!

California Pocket Mouse (*Chaetodipus californicus*)

Conservation Status: Least Concern

Description: Found from San Francisco down to the San Diego border and east to the Sierras, this little guy is a native Californian. It is quite common amongst coast scrub, chaparral, grassland and evergreen forests and is thus found in every region within Henry Cowell. It feeds primarily on grass seeds and the occasional insect that it can capture on the ground.

The California Pocket Mouse is a nocturnal animal and will sleep during the day in its burrow, venturing out at night to feed. It is preyed upon by coyotes, bobcats, owls and snakes. Like the Botta's Pocket Gopher, the Pocket Mouse gets its name by storing food in its cheek pouches.

Western Harvest Mouse (*Reithrodontomys megalotis*)

Conservation Status: Least Concern

Description: The Western Harvest Mouse is a nocturnal rodent that is native over most of the western United States. Brownish fur and a white belly covering a small round body help to distinguish the harvest mouse from other rodents. The Western Harvest Mouse will be less active under a full moon, preferring the complete cover of darkness as an ally to its stealth abilities to find seeds and insects without becoming prey. That being said, it is a

common dietary component of most predators. The Western Harvest Mouse has been known to store seeds and other food in underground vaults, which is the trait that gives the Harvest mouse its name.

116

Deer mouse (*Peromyscus maniculatus*)

Conservation Status: Least Concern

Description: The Deer mouse has a broad range, from Alaska to South America. Most deer mice nest high in hollows of trees and are generally nocturnal. They are quite adaptable and are found in a vast array of ecological communities, including grasslands, chaparral and forests.

Deer mice have been a cause for concern lately as they are a vector of the Hantavirus. Almost all human cases of the Hantavirus have been as a result of contact with rodent excrement and the Deer Mouse has been documented as a host of the virus. It is not understood why the Deer Mouse and not all rodents act as carriers.

Hanta virus itself gets its name from the Hantan River in South Korea where it was first discovered in the late 1970's. The hantaviruses are a relatively new genus. The first outbreak occurred amongst several thousand United Nation soldiers stationed in Korea during the Korean War. It would take 25 years to discover the cause of that outbreak. In 1993 another outbreak was recorded in the southwestern United States and has spread into the Sierras including Yosemite National Park where eight new cases and three deaths were confirmed in August 2012.

Given the viruses' recent existence, our ability to defend its onslaught is equally new. Symptoms can become quite severe and even lead to death. For most the virus gives symptoms similar to a bad flu. It will incubate within an infected human for two to four weeks before displaying the typical flu like symptoms of fever, chills, nausea and back pain.

While the flu (called HFRS) is debilitating in and of itself, a patient with HFRS is at risk to actually have Hantavirus Pulmonary Syndrome (HPS). While the symptoms are almost indistinguishable at first, HPS can lead to cardiovascular shock and is often fatal. The good news is getting HPS itself is rare, the bad news is that it is fatal in 60% of the cases. This is what gives alarm to the medical community since the early symptoms of more typical flu viruses, Hanta flu (HFRS) and the potentially fatal HPS are very similar. If you suspect you have either, it's best to seek medical attention.

Pinyon Mouse (*Peromyscus truei*)

Conservation Status: Least Concern

Description: The Pinyon Mouse has one thing that makes it easily recognizable; it's very large ears for this moderately large mouse. It is a native of the south-western United States. It is also known as the Big-eared Cliff Mouse.

Dusky-footed woodrat (*Neotoma fuscipes*)

Conservation Status: Least Concern

Description: Another nocturnal rodent, the Dusky-footed Woodrat is commonly referred to as a packrat. This is because it is known to build large domed dens that can reach several feet high. The dens are near fortresses, being able to fend off the onslaught by a coyote or other predator who will give up before reaching their prey. They look very similar to the infamous rattus rattus, (the common black rat) and are distinguished from them by larger eyes and ears and furred tail.

It has been observed that the Dusky-footed Woodrat will intentionally place California Bay leaves around the edges of their nest. Biologists believe that somehow the Woodrat made the connection that the volatile oils in the Bay leaves, which are toxic to flea larvae, would help them control fleas in their nests.

Black Rat (*Rattus rattus*)

Conservation Status: Least Concern

Description: The Black Rat is a world traveler. Believed to have originated in India, they then spread to Egypt and throughout the Roman Empire, reaching England around the 1st century. With the advent of nautical voyages, the Black rat was spread from Europe to the rest of the world.

Given their populations can explode and the fact that they have no problem living in urban areas, the Black Rat has figured prominently and negatively throughout history. Perhaps their biggest claim to fame is in being tied to the Black Death, which killed nearly a quarter of the world's population, roughly 100 million people at that time, though some estimates double that figure. The death rate in some countries, like Iraq, Iran and Syria was almost a third of the population. Forty percent of Egypt's population was reduced and an astounding 50% of Paris citizens perished because of it. Occurring in the 14th century, it is considered one of the most devastating pandemics in human history.

It took Europe nearly 150 years to recover from the plague and had profound religious, social and economic effects that dramatically changed the course of European history. It led to religious persecution, targeted mostly at the Jewish population who were blamed for the crisis.

Art of the Black Plague Period

The Black Rat is a carrier not only for the bubonic plaque, but typhus, toxoplasmosis and trichinosis. It is a complex pest and difficult to control due to its high intelligence and extreme adaptability.

California vole (*Microtus californicus*)

Conservation Status: Least Concern

Description: A vole is a small rodent that while resembling a mouse, has a stouter body, rounded head, and a shorter, hairy tail. The California vole is one of 155 species of the vole family. They reach sexual maturity in just one month and can have up to 10 litters per year. Under the right ecological conditions, they have achieved exponential growth.

A single pregnant vole can produce more than a hundred active voles in less than a year. Given a normal ecosystem, their knack for creating lots of off-spring is offset by their many predators, including hawks, raccoons and even house cats.

Carnivores (*Carnivora*)

Coyote (*Canis latrans*)

Conservation Status: Least Concern

"Whenever the pressure of our complex city life thins my blood and numbs my brain, I seek relief in the trail; and when I hear the coyote wailing to the yellow dawn, my cares fall from me - I am happy." – Hamlin Garland.

Description: Despite being extensively hunted, the coyote is one of the few mammals that have increased their range of habitation, originally the western half of North America and now the entire United States and Canada. This may be in part to the equally extensive hunting of wolves and their unique ability to co-exist in urban and suburban areas. The extent that they do coexist is surprising. One seven year study found there were up to 2,000 coyotes living in the greater Chicago area. Their adaptation is almost ninja like as while they adapted well to living within densely populated urban environments, they do so in a manner that is completely hidden from the humans they live amongst. The study also found that urban coyotes outlived their wilderness counterparts.

Outside of urban areas, coyotes are a big problem for ranchers of sheep, goat and cattle. According to the 2004 National Agricultural Statistics Service, coyotes were responsible for over 60% of sheep deaths in that year, some 134,000 sheep. As a result of the uneasy relationship in the suburban environments, they are actively hunted. The U.S. government routinely traps, shoots or poisons some 90,000 coyotes that range within livestock areas.

The coyote is a species of canine and primarily hunt in pairs or occasionally in larger groups. Typical packs are made of six closely related adults, juveniles and young. They live about 10 years in the wild but up to 18 in captivity.

The calls of a coyote are amongst the most awe inspiring animal sounds in nature. Typically a series of howls, yips, yelps and barks, the coyote call is a chorus of wilderness song, usually cutting the stark silence of the night. The calls echo amongst the hillsides and fills the land for miles with their series of howls and yips, dropping to some final notes and then as quickly as it began, the calls end.

Coyotes are prevalent in Native American folklore, appearing as prominent figures within creation myths at the beginning of time and as tricksters and/or heroes in current times. Whether seen as clever tricksters or a creature able to achieve the impossible, the coyote is well respected.

Gray Fox (*Urocyon cinereoargenteus*)

Conservation Status: Least Concern

Description: The Gray Fox has been with us for over 3.6 million years according to fossil evidence found in Arizona. Given the dramatic and

complete changes in the environments in which it lived, through ice ages, jungle like conditions and present day climes, this is a pretty amazing statement.

The Gray Fox is nocturnal, monogamous and comes from the same family as coyotes and dogs. They are omnivorous and prefer to hunt alone. They are fairly adept at making a diet of brush and jackrabbits, as well as voles and other rodents. In desert areas where a meat diet is infrequent, the Gray Fox will adapt to insects and fruits for sustenance. Kits (young foxes) will begin to hunt as early as three months and can hunt on their own at four months. Once the kits reach sexual maturity, they will leave home, venturing on their own to start the cycle anew.

Raccoon (*Procyon lotor*)

Conservation Status: Least Concern

Description: Raccoons started life in deciduous and mixed forests but with the advent of humans, they have adapted to live amongst us. Their range extends throughout North America and beyond to Europe, Russia and even Japan. Raccoons are increasing in urban areas and exhibit less fear around humans than other mammals. Hunting and getting caught in traffic are the two most common causes of death. It has been found in areas where hunt-

ing is common as an eradication method, the Raccoons adaptability extends to a higher rate of reproduction to compensate.

Raccoons are one of the smarter mammals that do live among and around us. A study done in 1908 by H. B. Davis found raccoons could open 11 of 13 complex locks he set out for them in fewer than 10 tries. Further studies have shown that raccoons are not only able to understand abstract principles, but could do so as quickly as a Rhesus monkey and could retain the memory of what they learned for three years.

Raccoons are nocturnal and omnivorous, eating a variety of plants, insects, worms, and easily caught fish and bird eggs. Many have observed raccoons washing their meals before eating; however it is not completely certain to scientists as to why they do this.

Raccoons are known carriers of rabies and care should be taken when around them, especially those that do not show fear of humans. That being said, with rabies vaccination policies and awareness, there has only been one documented human fatality due the transmission of rabies from a raccoon bite.

Long-tailed Weasel (*Mustela frenata*)

Conservation Status: Least Concern

Description: The Long-tailed Weasel is a member of the Mustelidae family, which make up a group of small active predators that are long, slender and have short legs. The Long-tailed Weasel is the largest of this family. They are found throughout North America and as far south as northern South America, living in rocky dens or abandoned burrows.

The Long-tailed Weasel will feed on animals much larger than themselves, including rabbits. Their technique is to strike in rapid fashion, biting any part of the body they can grab ahold of, climbing onto the body and digging in with their feet will continue to attack until they can inflict a lethal bite to the neck.

For night identification, the weasel's eyes will glow a bright emerald green if caught in the beam of a flashlight. During the day, their long slender body covered in an auburn brown fur makes the weasel easy to spot. The other distinction is the black tip of their tail.

Striped Skunk (*Mephitis mephitis*)

Conservation Status: Least Concern

Description: Oh, the beloved skunk, one of the few animals that invoke the question, "What's that smell?" on forest drives. The skunk is widespread throughout the United States and Canada and is one of the most recognized mammals with its black fur with double white stripe. It prefers ecosystems of woodlands, grasslands and agricultural areas.

Skunks are omnivorous, eating mainly insects but also earthworms and even honeybees. They will eat small animals such as frogs and voles as well as berries and other wild fruit. In urban areas, they can become a problem for pet owners who leave food out for the cat or dog. They have also been known to dig up lawns looking for grubs and worms. Skunks typically hunt during twilight hours of dusk and dawn, retiring to its burrow during the day.

As to who preys on the skunk, most of the typical predators don't due to the skunk's ability to fend for itself using its foul smell. The noted exception to this is the Great Horned Owl, which lacks a sense of smell.

The widely known defense mechanism of the skunk is its ability to spray a foul smell from its anal glands. This chemical, a mixture of sulfur containing chemicals collectively called mercaptans, produce a highly offensive smell that is unique but has similar qualities to rotten eggs and burnt rubber. It is powerful enough to ward off bears and can cause skin irritation, temporary blindness and can even permanently stain house paint. The skunk can aim and disperse the chemical with a high degree of accuracy up to 10 feet. It is detectable by the human nose for up to a mile radius from where it was dispersed.

That being said, skunks will use this weapon as a last resort as they carry a limited quantity of five to six uses that requires 10 days to replenish. A skunk's first defense is to hiss and stamp its feet, followed by placing their tails high in the air. If you haven't gotten the message that you've upset the skunk and should run at this point, be prepared to get doused with skunk odor.

A Few Skunk Jokes (that truly stink):

Baby Skunk: "Mother, can i have a chemistry set?"

Mother Skunk: "What! And smell up the house?"

There were two skunks, one named In and one named Out. Once, Out went in and said to Out, "Bring In in." So Out went out, got In, and they went in. Their mother was happy to see them. She asked Out, "How did you find In so fast?" And Out said, "Instincts."

Q: Where does a skunk sit in a church?

A: In a Pew

Mountain Lion (*Puma concolor*)

Conservation Status: Least Concern

Description: Cougar, puma, mountain lion and catamount are all synonymous names for top predator of Wilder Ranch State Park. The mountain lion in general has the greatest range of any large terrestrial mammal in the Western Hemisphere and is found from the Yukon in Canada to the southern Andes of Chile. It is an adaptable animal and is found in every American habitat type. It is the second heaviest cat in the Western Hemisphere, the jaguar being the first. The mountain lion is a true carnivore, eating only meat.

The mountain lion is a nocturnal animal and uses a stalk and ambush method to attack its prey. It will typically prey on Mule Deer but has been known to attack domestic animals as well, such as cattle, horses and sheep. That being said, it is typically reclusive when it comes to humans and will avoid them under most circumstances. It is territorial, the size of which depending on the abundance of food within it. Besides eating large game, it also hunts rodents and even insects to augment a bigger catch.

Bobcat (*Felis rufus*)

Conservation Status: Least Concern

Description: Bobcats are the smallest of four species of medium sized wildcats referred to as lynxes. It is an adaptable predator found throughout the United States. It can be found primarily in the forested areas of Wilder Ranch State Park. They are solitary, able hunters, using a spotted coat as camouflage. It feeds mainly on rabbits and hares but will not pass by smaller prey such as insects or small rodents. Like the skunk, Bobcat's hunt mainly at dusk and dawn. There have been reported cases of Bobcats successfully killing larger animals such as deer.

Mating among the bobcats is a pursuit of the male. During courtship, the pair may undertake a number of different behaviors, such as bumping, chasing and ambushing as well as screams and hisses. The female will raise the young of one to six pups by herself after about 60 days of gestation. The pups are born with eyes closed, opening them after ten days. They begin exploring their surroundings at four weeks and within five months will accompany their mother on hunts. They will begin to hunt on their own by the fall of their first year.

In Wilder, the Cougar and Coyote are the Bobcats only known predator. However outside the park, bobcats are regularly hunted. Despite this, their numbers have remained steadily resilient.

Harbor Seal (*Phoca vitulina*)

Conservation Status: Least Concern

Description: When one ponders that the Harbor Seal is a mammal, as are humans, it is astounding. Yes, they breathe air, feed and give birth in manners common to all mammals. However they have no legs, either to walk upright or on all fours and of the highest peculiarity is the fact that they live most comfortably in the marine coastlines of the Northern Hemisphere. We swim in the ocean, some of us live near the ocean, but here is a mammal that spends its life primarily in the ocean.

Harbor Seals can be brown, gray or tan and have a distinctive V-shaped nostril. They can weigh up to 290 pounds and live up to 35 years (though only females live that long, males tend to live up to 25 years). They tend to hang out in sheltered coves with rocky sea mounts. A female will bear a single pup, which can swim and dive within hours of birth. They are often confused with sea lions. Harbor seals have a smooth head while sea lions have "ears". There is a global population of between 5-6 million and are on the rise as nations have agreed on bans to hunt the Harbor Seal.

Pups initially feed on their mother's fat-rich milk but will quickly become predators of fish, shrimp, crabs and mussels living within their ecosystem. Adults have been known to attack and eat various seabirds as well. The birthing process occurs onshore and like humans, gestation is 9 months. Breeding in California occurs from March to May.

Sea Otter (*Enhydra lutris*)

Conservation Status: Endangered

Description: Amazingly, the Long-tailed Weasel and the Sea Otter both come from the same "weasel family" Mustelidae. Unlike the terrestrial weasel cousins, the Sea Otter has chosen marine coastlines as its territory. The Sea Otter can be found in coastal waters on both sides of the northern Pacific Ocean.

Sea Otters forage the sea floor preying mainly on sea urchins, mollusks and other crustaceans. A familiar tapping sound may occasionally be heard in the waters where Sea Otters live. They will place a shell on their bellies and then use a rock to crack the shell open. This trait is unique and makes the Sea Otter one of the few mammals besides primates to use tools as part of their behavior. The Sea Otter is considered a keystone species, keeping the highly reproductive sea urchin population in check, which if left unmanaged would extensively damage kelp forest ecosystems.

When Spaniards and later US Citizens came to the shores where Sea Otters lived, the otter enjoyed a robust population estimated at up to 300,000 members worldwide and 16,000 in California. Their pelts were in very high demand during the 18th century. In Oregon, the otter was hunted to extinction in that state by 1906. In 1911 the world Sea Otter population fell to just 1,000-2,000 individuals living worldwide. Conservation measures since have allowed the population of otters to increase but they are still considered an endangered species, one of the few in Wilder. As of 2007, a census counted 3,026 Sea Otters living in California. Recently, it has been observed that the Sea Otter has declined to some extent as of 2010. It is unknown exactly why this is occurring, suspect causes include toxic bacteria in the shellfish as a result of human waste products ending in the oceans.

Hoofed Animals (*Artiodactyla*)

Mule Deer (*Odocoileus hemionus*)

Conservation Status: Least Concern

Description: Mule Deer, including the California Mule Deer, are quite common and easily spotted by viewing their white rump with a black tip. They range from Mexico to Alaska and as far east as the Rocky Mountains. Most will be found foraging around dawn and dusk but may also forage during the full moon. They are known to bed down in the same area or in temporary beds. Repeated beds will be often scratched level and are about the size of a washtub. Temporary beds are more easily spotted as multiple flattened grassy areas. Mule deer rarely stray far from either water or forage and bed down within easy walking distance of both.

Young forage in groups while mature bucks travel alone or with other bucks. Mule deer are herbivores, and eat seasonally available plants. They will eat most woody vegetation, including Douglas fir, but little grass. In season they will eat acorns and wild berries.

Top predators beyond humans are mountain lions, coyotes and where present black bears. They have little defense mechanisms and rely almost exclusively on speed and alertness to avoid predation. The top two enemies of deer involve human interaction, hunting and automobiles.

California Golden Bear, California Grizzly
(*Ursus arctos horribilis*)

Conservation Status: Extinct in California, Threatened nationally

Description: Grizzly bears enjoyed a range from Alaska to Mexico and as far east as Hudson Bay. Today, the Grizzly is only found in Alaska and occasionally in Canada. Ironically, the Grizzly bear is the principle figure of the California State flag. The last known grizzly in this state was shot in 1922 by a rancher in Fresno.

Prior to human intrusion into the grizzly's range, the bear thrived in valleys and coastal slopes of California. Some researchers conclude that the grizzly was more abundant in California than any other state. By 1850 however, the California population exploded from 1,500 residents to 300,000, due exclusively to the Gold Rush. The gold miners both respected the grizzly and found them to be a threatening nuisance. In California as well as other states that grew in population, the grizzlies and civilization did not mix well. Unlike other mammals that faced similar threats from humans, grizzlies stood their ground and defended their territory rather than running to safer ground. This was a reasonable assumption as prior to humans, they were the top of the food chain, but it would prove to become a costly trait for the Grizzly. Within 75 years of the Gold Rush, every grizzly would be hunted and killed or otherwise fled the state.

130

Pronghorn (*Antilocapra var.*)

Conservation Status: Limited in California, no longer present in Wilder, Least Concern nationally

At one point, there were five species of pronghorn when humans first entered North America, now all but one, A. Americana is extinct. The pronghorn were one of the hunted animals of the Ohlone Native Americans. Today, pronghorn can be found in the northeast corner of California and in small to large pockets throughout the western United States.

Pronghorns are a migratory animal whose paths have been pinched off as humans inhabited them. As migration corridors were cut off, the pronghorn suffered as a result. As well, the pronghorn was actively hunted. In the 1920's the population was hunted to near extinction with only 13,000 animals left. Today, through both habitat protection and hunting restrictions, their numbers are closer to 500,000 to 1,000,000. Still habitat fragmentation will likely keep the pronghorn from returning to Wilder in the near future.

Surfing

Four Mile Beach

Four Mile is so named because it is located about four miles north of Santa Cruz. It has a good long beach, dubbed the "Florida Mile" by locals, a reference to the number of tourists that frequent the beach. It does have rippable surf, breaking to the right. The bottom is classified as a "rock reef, semi gnarly" by Surfline.com and ranks a 7 on their "Perfect-O-Meter (1 being Lake Erie). Best swells are NW, W, and WSW and the best tide is incoming to high. A good all season surf spot for intermediate to expert surfers and is listed as being a "5-Moderate" on the bicep burn, mainly because of the swimming needed to get out to the waves.

One caution that is mirrored by everyone, although it has better parking and is an easier walk than Three Mile Beach, it is notorious for thievery in the parking lot, so hide your goodies.

Three Mile Beach

Three Mile Beach has many of the same characteristics of Four Mile Beach but does have notable distinctions. For starters, Three Mile is, well, three miles north of Santa Cruz rather than four miles. (That is a distinction, albeit a rather obvious one, let's move on). The parking capacity for Three Mile is far less than Four Mile and while the beach is less crowded, it can still be crowded on weekends.

The other biggest factor besides parking is it's a farther walk to the surf, about 15-30 minutes, which can be good if you are trying to find a more private spot. Both beaches share the same rocky bottom, semi gnarly characteristics. Like Four Mile, the best swells are NW, W, and WSW and the best tide is incoming to high. Swells have been described as quirky oscillating from skunk like to god like.

Again, parking lot theft is an issue so hide your stuff.

Closing Remarks

Writing a comprehensive guide about a mere 7000 acre park turned out to be much larger project than I originally anticipated. The fact that it did become a larger project is a testimony to the diversity that is packed into this small area.

I picked Wilder because I liked the park. What I learned along the way is that Wilder Ranch State Park is rich in a history that reaches to the Ice Age and covers every major milestone within California's history. I learned that there are a whole clan of volunteers that are truly passionate about making the visitors stay (their customer) as enjoyable as possible. I learned that it took a band of concerned citizens to keep the land of Wilder and its dairy ranching history from being wiped out and turned into a track of seventies style homes. Most of all, I learned in a fuller way why I wrote this book, to help increase adoption of Wilder to California History and to the State Parks as whole so that others could enjoy this amazing California treasure.

I do hope that is some small way, that goal is reached.

Take care, God bless and most of all thanks!

Eric Henze

About the Author

Eric Henze began his writing career at the age of twelve with a sci fi short titled "5:15", tackling a plot around a timepiece that could end the world. His passion for hiking started in Sedona, Arizona where he lived in his youth. It expanded to peak bagging in the Sierra Nevada Mountains and then the Andes of South America, where he lived as a Peace Corp volunteer for two years, climbing many of the peaks of Ecuador and Peru. A highlight was climbing Sangay, an active volcano that often shoots VW size rocks at climbers to maintain their attention. In his own words, "It was a delight".

His passions for writing, hiking and adventure have led to a series of guidebooks for both the National Park Service and the California State Parks. A portion of the proceeds of all of his books go towards directly supporting these parks. His latest work is titled "A Family Guide to the Grand Circle National Parks", a family oriented travel guide for seven national parks in the Southwestern United States.

135

About Friends of Santa Cruz State Park

Friends of Santa Cruz State Parks is an entrepreneurial nonprofit sustaining the legacy of our state parks and beaches. Through an innovative partnership with California State Parks, and by leveraging local community support, Friends has provided millions of dollars of funding for educational programs, visitor services and capital projects.

Wilder Ranch State Park is supported by Friends of Santa Cruz State Parks through funding for a variety of projects and ongoing needs, such as:

- Capital improvements, including a recent new roof for the Meder House
- Special events, including the Heritage Harvest Festival, Old-fashioned 4th of July and Holidays @ the Ranch
- Interpretive and educational programming
- Docent and volunteer support

Founded in 1976, Friends is passionately dedicated to the preservation of our spectacular natural environment and rich cultural history. Friends also operates six ParkStores, offering nature- and history-themed merchandise for sale to benefit local parks and beaches. ParkStore locations include Natural Bridges, New Brighton, Santa Cruz Mission, Seacliff, Wilder Ranch and Online. Learn more about Friends of Santa Cruz State Parks at ThatsMyPark. org or via Facebook, Twitter, YouTube and Pinterest.

Selected Reading

- Wilder Ranch State Park Vegetation Map, September 2002 Prepared by Inventory, Monitoring, and Assessment Program, Natural Resources Division
- California Department of Parks and Recreation, Wilder Ranch State Park Inventory, Monitoring, and Assessment Project
- California Department of Parks and Recreation Natural Resources Division Small and Meso Mammal Monitoring at Wilder Ranch State Park July 2002 By Pat Gilbert Research Analyst
- Wilder Ranch State Park Cookbook 1870's to the 1920's by Pat Kennedy
- Unofficial Site: Good overall site for horse enthusiasts that want to explore Wilder Ranch State Park (www.wilderstatepark.com)
- Wilder Ranch State Park - Official Site: California State Parks official site (http://www.parks.ca.gov/?page_id=549)
- Friends of Santa Cruz State Parks website features much information on the parks and beaches of Santa Cruz. (http://www.thatsmypark.org/)
- Surfline.com website features great information for surfers (http://www.surfline.com)
- Santa Cruz Bird Club website has tons of birding information for the Santa Cruz region (http://santacruzbirdclub.org)
- Lime Kiln Legacies is both a website and book devoted to Santa Cruz's lime kiln industry
- Sandy Lydon is one of the most knowledgeable historians when it comes to Santa Cruz. He regularly gives talks on various subjects within the area.
- Bay Area Hiker website has many hikes outlined, including Wilder Ranch State Park (http://www.bahiker.com/)

Photo Attributes

Attributions and permissions given where indicated.

Cover Photos

- Friends of Santa Cruz State Parks and Ken Sievers.

Title Page

- Wilder Creamery, by permission of CA State Park Archives

In order of appearance.

General Information

- The Wilder Ranch perserved farmhouse, Grey3k, CC-BY-3.0
- Parking: Imagery©2013 AMBAG, DigitalGlobe, GeoEye, USDA Farm Service Agency, Map data ©2013 Google
- Entrance, by permission of wilderstatepark.com
- Wilder RR, by permission of Ken Sievers
- Fee sign, by Eric Henze
- Cat Granary, by permission of Ken Sievers
- Wilder Ranch Cabin, by permission of Ken Sievers
- Docents, by permission of Ken Sievers
- Blacksmithing by permission of Ken Sievers

Geology

- Aerial view of Wilder Ranch State Park, by S. Stringall, copyright Gone Beyond Guides

Area History

- Mission San Jose Natives, from Mission San Juan Capistrano: A Pocket History and Tour Guide, PD - US
- Abalone badges, courtesy of the Muwekma Ohlone Tribe
- Wilder Creamery, by permission of CA State Park Archives
- Early sunrise, by permission of CA State Park Archives
- Pelton Wheel, by permission of Ken Sievers
- Adams Creek Lime Kiln Ruins, by Eric Henze

Wilder Stories - The People of Wilder

- Levi Baldwin, by permission of CA State Park Archives
- Baldwin Stamp, by permission of CA State Park Archives
- DD Wilder Creamery, by permission of CA State Park Archives
- Delos D Wilder, by permission of CA State Park Archives
- Melvin Wilder, by permission of CA State Park Archives
- Melvin and Lettie Wilder, by permission of CA State Park Archives
- Ethel Wilder, by permission of CA State Park Archives
- Wilder Kids, by permission of CA State Park Archives
- DR Wilder, by permission of CA State Park Archives
- Polo Scene, by permission of CA State Park Archives
- Moroto Investment Company Plan, page 42, courtesy Friends of Santa Cruz State Parks
- Moroto Investment Company Plan, page 60, courtesy Friends of Santa Cruz State Parks
- Moroto Investment Company Plan, page 51, courtesy Friends of Santa Cruz State Parks

Wilder Ranch Tour

- Buildings of the Historic Wilder Ranch Complex, Docent Manual, by Cynthia Mathews
- Bolcoff Adobe, by permission of CA State Park Archives
- Meder House, by permission of CA State Park Archives
- Melvin Wilder Victorian, by permission of CA State Park Archives
- Horse Barn, by permission of CA State Park Archives
- Workshop and Bunkhouse, by permission of CA State Park Archives
- Cow Barn, by permission of CA State Park Archives
- Inside Cow Barn, by permission of CA State Park Archives
- Loading Hay into Cow Barn, by permission of CA State Park Archives
- Garage, by permission of CA State Park Archives
- The Bungalow, by permission of CA State Park Archives
- Creamery, by permission of CA State Park Archives
- Various Outbuildings, by permission of CA State Park Archives

Trails

- Bracken Ferns, by permission of Ken Sievers
- Natural Bridge, CA State Park Archives
- Ohlone Bluff, Greg3k, CC-BY-3.0
- View of Wilder Ranch, by permission of Ken Sievers
- Wilder Ridge Loop Trail, CC-BY-3.0
- Dairy Trail, CC-BY-3.0
- Zane Grey Cutoff, CC-BY-3.0
- Engelsmans Loop, CC-BY-3.0
- Wild Boar Trail, CC-BY-3.0
- Moth, by permission of Ken Sievers
- Twin Oaks Trail, CC-BY-3.0
- Horsemans Trail, by permission of www.wilderstatepark.com
- Enchanted Loop Trail, by permission of Ken Sievers
- Baldwin Loop Trail, CC-BY-3.0
- Woodcutter's Trail, CC-BY-3.0
- Chinquapin Trail, CC-BY-3.0
- Eucalyptus Trail, CC-BY-3.0
- Long Meadow Trail, by permission of santa-cruz-agent.com

Flora

- Sand Verbana, by permission of Jane Huber/Bay Area Hiker
- Beach Bur, by Eric in SF, CC-BY-SA-3.0
- Sea Rocket, by Jürgen Howaldt, CC-BY-SA-2.0-DE
- Oenothera cheiranthifolia, by Noah Elhardt, CC-BY-SA-3.0,2.5,2.0,1.0
- Carpobrotuschilensis, taken at Thornbill Beach, Point Saint Mugu State Park, PD US NPS
- Distichlis spicata; Salt Grass, by R.C. Brody, PD
- Eriophyllum staechadifolium, by Tom Hilton, CC-BY-2.0
- Flowers of Erodium malacoides, by Alvesgaspar, CC-BY-SA-3.0
- Eriogonumlatifolium, by Gordon Leppig & Andrea J. Pickart, PD US FWS
- Typha latifolia, by Bogdan, CC-BY-SA-3.0-migrated
- Brennnessel 1 , by Uwe H. Friese, CC-BY-SA-3.0-migrated
- Urtica dioica, by Frank Vincentz, CC-BY-SA-3.0-migrated
- Schoenoplectus acutus at Humboldt Bay National Wildlife Refuge Complex, California, USA, By, Gordon Leppig & Andrea J. Pickart, PD US FWS
- Red alder leaves (Alnus rubra), by Hadal, PD US BLM
- Alnus rubra , by Walter Siegmund, CC-BY-SA-3.0-migrated
- Salix lasiolepis, by William & Wilma Follette, PD USDA
- Sambucus racemosa, by Frank Vincentz, CC-BY-SA-3.0-migrated
- Lithocarpus densiflorus leaves, by Joseph O'Brien, CC-BY-3.0-US
- Photo of an acorn, by Mark Osgatharp, PD-user
- Pacific Madrone (Arbutus menziesii), by NaJina McEnany, CC-BY-SA-2.5
- Pacific Madrone (Arbutus menziesii) blossom, by Stephen Lea, PD-user

Fauna

Surfing